I0114346

Steps to Success

PETER DORAN

Esquire Publications
1400 Hwy 41, #2503
Inverness, FL 34451
www.esquirepublications.com
Tel: 1-800-501-7640

"Steps to Success"

Edited By: Georgia Editing Service, LLC.
Book and Cover Design By
Designs Unparallel, LLC
www.designsunparallel.net

Copyright© 2021 by Peter Doran

This book is a work of nonfiction. All rights reserved. Printed in the United States of America. No part of this book may be used or reproduced in any manner whatsoever without written permission from the publisher.

Library of Congress Cataloging-in-Publication Data

Library of Congress Control Number: 2021914223

ISBN: 9781737691808

Steps to Success

I have been blessed with the luck of the draw to stumble upon my passions during my first career by starting my life working in the military.

This allowed me to find my passion by starting out in communications for military intelligence section. This was interesting work that was different every day and challenging at times, but I found myself looking for more. I found that others in my section have found their niche in life, and that it is either what they have done for their whole work life or something they would like to do. I felt different than that; I was looking for more out of life than just doing my job and going home.

I found myself observing people in other positions and found that there were three main types of people to interact with inside the occupations they held. There were people that loved what they did and found the sweet spot in life to balance and harmonize with them and their career. There were people that would just do their job and be happy with the ones around them. This type of people does not enjoy the work, but instead enjoy the types of people they surrounded themselves with. There were also people that were unhappy with everything. Coming to work was a chore, and at the very least they appeared to be dissatisfied with every phase of their situation. At a young age, I experimented with different positions in the military before I found that an instructor position fit my personality to a tee. I stopped thinking that my career was work, and instead realized that this was a part of me that I enjoyed in all the phases of my life. I spent the remainder of my career in training and education for the military.

What I am offering will save yourself wasted time, effort, and frustration. This is an opportunity to start off on the right path from the beginning. Maybe you find yourself like I did, in a career where you should be happy, but you are missing something or maybe you just are looking for more and want some initial ideas. This guide will turn your passion into your profession with tips on becoming successful in your own way.

Let's Start with The Findings

While working in workforce development, I have found that there are three different ways that people find their ultimate position. If you compare this to how you can arrive at any destination it would equate to taking the train – following the road – floating on the river.

Now take a look at which path you have taken and what strengths you have from your journey.

Taking the Train

This is the formal education route, some people know what they want from an early age, these people have started their adult life in an education system focused on the career path that they knew fit them best. They most likely have found this career at an early age from job shadowing a relative or a local employer or took some interest interviews or even had some experience from volunteering or other activities the lead them to this career. They will have the strengths of becoming subject matter experts in a shorter amount of time because their interest will have them focused on learning more about that career. If you are on this path, I recommend expanding your knowledge in many possible ways. Also, think of outside the box ways. For instance, you could volunteer for events or be on boards to become a subject matter expert that you didn't expect.

Following the Road

This is the route of working in an industry and working your way up. Initially, they start in an entry level position sometimes without any formal education and continue to work their way up to the ultimate position. They have a mix of education and experience. The experience is their strength. They understand what it is like to be in an entry level position. Also, they know how the industry works inside and out, not from a book, but from life experiences. If you are on this path, I recommend finding credentials in your career to demonstrate on paper how much of an expert you are.

Floating on the River

This is the route where the person is taking a fatalistic approach and allowing opportunities to guide their path. They may have some education and in many careers the education is not directly associated with the career. Their strength is being a jack of all trades, where their broad experiences have allowed them to learn about many different experiences that they can bring to the ultimate career. They are generally more flexible people and willing to learn. If you are on this path, document your success on paper of how much of an expert you are, this could include a recommendation or thanks from peers, mentors, or co-workers.

In this self help guide we will start with the basics. We will discover yourself, not only by taking an assessment and finding your personality to and the best matches, but we will also professionally describe what your experiences and qualities are regardless of your background. Then, we will create a sample application that is included in the guide and create a resume focusing on the different skills that you listed on your application. Also, you will gain understanding on how we can also use a cover letter and possibly a portfolio to incorporate the missing pieces that are not listed on the application and resume, that you can modify for each position that you are seeking. Once we are prepared, we will understand how we can find the available positions and walk through the proper steps to apply for these positions and how to conduct ourselves on the interview and on the job itself.

This guide is focused on finding the free resources to all of the systems we will be discussing, because regardless of why we are searching for a new career the last thing a job seeker can afford is more expense during this challenging time.

Remember as we are taking each step, that now we all have a new job, as a salesperson. This is where the most successfully sales tactic for us is to know our product, understand how it can be utilized in each market, and the value. Remember, *ATTITUDE IS EVERYTHING* with the presentation. Sell yourself the best way you can!

Know Yourself Assessment - Interest Profiler

Know your Personality Type with the Holland Code

Online Resource: O*Net Interest Profiler http://www.mynextmove.org/explore/ip

One way of exploring careers is by looking at occupations according to occupational interest. John Holland conducted research that divided job seekers into six broad personality type categories:

• REALISTIC • INVESTIGATIVE • ARTISTIC • SOCIAL • ENTERPRISING • CONVENTIONAL

All types have both positive and negative qualities, and none are better than the others. The Holland Code is a generalization, and not likely to be an exact fit. This condensed survey is not intended to be as accurate or comprehensive as a full instrument. Completing this survey might help you identify the cluster(s) of occupations in which you would have the most interest and get the most satisfaction, and it will give you a place to start your career exploration.

Step One: Circle the number of all items below that are appealing to you - leave the rest blank.

1. Planting and growing crops
2. Solving math problems
3. Being in a play
4. Studying other cultures
5. Talking to people at a party
6. Working with computers
7. Working on cars or lawnmowers
8. Astronomy
9. Drawing or painting
10. Going to church
11. Working on a sales campaign
12. Using a cash register
13. Carpentry
14. Physics
15. Foreign language
16. Working with youth

17. Buying clothes for a store
18. Working from nine to five
19. Setting type for a printing job
20. Using a chemistry set
21. Reading fiction or plays
22. Helping people with problems
23. Selling life insurance
24. Typing reports
25. Driving a truck
26. Working in a lab
27. Playing a musical instrument
28. Making new friends
29. Leading a group
30. Following a budget
31. Fixing electrical appliances
32. Building rocket models

33. Writing stories or poetry
34. Attending sports events
35. Making your opinions heard
36. Using business machines
37. Building things
38. Doing puzzles
39. Fashion design
40. Belonging to a club/organization
41. Giving talks or speeches
42. Keeping detailed records
43. Wildlife biology
44. Using science to get answers
45. Going to concerts or the theater
46. Working with the elderly
47. Salespeople
48. Filing letters and reports

Step Two: On the chart below, again circle the numbers of the items which appealed to you. Then count the number for each row and write the number in the box to the left. The three highest categories are the clusters in which you have the most interest, and their corresponding labels are your Holland Code. For example, if you scored highest in Social, and second highest in Artistic, and third highest in Enterprising your Holland Code would be "SAE." This is where you will concentrate your career exploration efforts.

R = REALISTIC	1	7	13	19	25	31	37	43
I = INVESTIGATIVE	2	8	14	20	26	32	38	44
A = ARTISTIC	3	9	15	21	27	33	39	45
S = SOCIAL	4	10	16	22	28	34	40	46
E = ENTERPRISING	5	11	17	23	29	35	41	47
C = CONVENTIONAL	6	12	18	24	30	36	42	48

Highest Score: _____ Second Highest Score: _____ Third Highest Score: _____
My Holland Code: _____

Career and Job Search Information

Search Using Your Holland Code

Online Resource: *O*Net Data - https://www.onetonline.org/*

Browse by O*NET Data

O*NET Data descriptors are categories of occupational information collected and available for O*NET-SOC occupations. Each descriptor contains more specific elements with data ratings.

[Interests ▾] [Go]

Interests

Preferences for work environments and outcomes.

Want to discover your interests? Take the O*NET Interest Profiler at My Next Move.

Realistic — Realistic occupations frequently involve work activities that include practical, hands-on problems and solutions. They often deal with plants, animals, and real-world materials like wood, tools, and machinery. Many of the occupations require working outside, and do not involve a lot of paperwork or working closely with others.

Investigative — Investigative occupations frequently involve working with ideas, and require an extensive amount of thinking. These occupations can involve searching for facts and figuring out problems mentally.

Artistic — Artistic occupations frequently involve working with forms, designs and patterns. They often require self-expression and the work can be done without following a clear set of rules.

Social — Social occupations frequently involve working with, communicating with, and teaching people. These occupations often involve helping or providing service to others.

Enterprising — Enterprising occupations frequently involve starting up and carrying out projects. These occupations can involve leading people and making many decisions. Sometimes they require risk taking and often deal with business.

Conventional — Conventional occupations frequently involve following set procedures and routines. These occupations can include working with data and details more than with ideas. Usually there is a clear line of authority to follow.

- *Click on the highest Holland interest you have.*
- *Click on careers that you would like to know more about.*

4	21-1092.00	Probation Officers and Correctional Treatment Specialists
4	39-9032.00	Recreation Workers
4	29-1125.00	Recreational Therapists
4	21-1015.00	Rehabilitation Counselors
4	25-2058.00	Special Education Teachers, Secondary School
4	13-1151.00	Training and Development Specialists
4	25-3041.00	Tutors
5	25-2059.01	Adapted Physical Education Specialists

Labor Market Information is a key ingredient to understanding the workplace and the dynamics which influence job search and career choices. It can help you to evaluate options and consider opportunities. That information, coupled with an awareness of your own interests, likes, and dislikes, will give you a sense of direction. You can further define that direction into a goal by identifying the skills you have or are willing to develop. Here are more ways to find out more about careers.

Another option to find careers is to review the related occupations at the bottom of a career. This could be to increase your pay, find more available options or just get a change of pace.

Online Resource: *Career One Stop - http://www.careeronestop.org/*

careeronestop
your source for car
Sponsored by the U.S. Depart

Explore Careers ▼   F

Search Careers

- Select Explore Careers
- Type Occupation
- Select State

Online Resource: *My Next Move - https://www.mynextmove.org/*

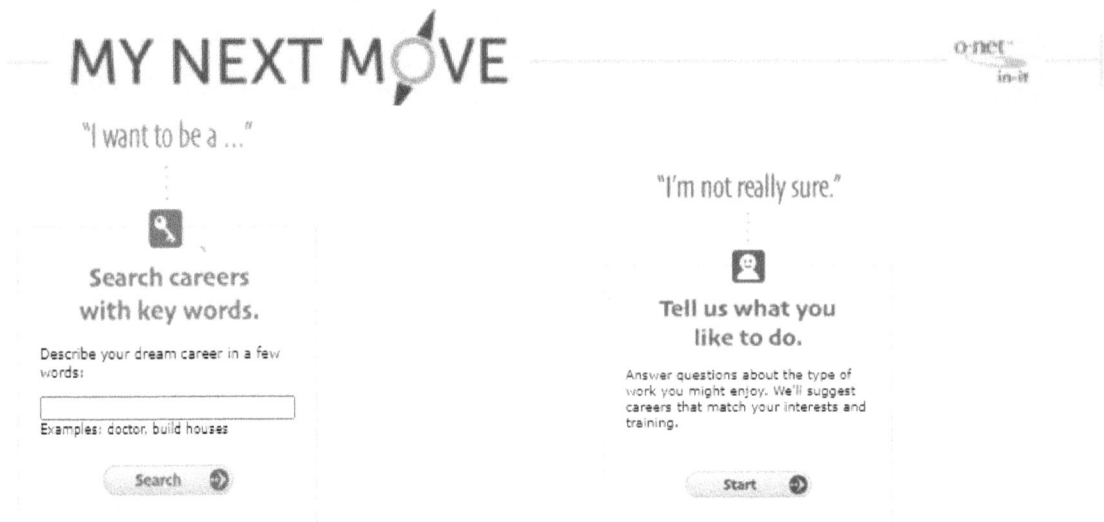

MY NEXT MOVE   o-net
                                                in-it

"I want to be a ..."

🔍

Search careers
with key words.

Describe your dream career in a few words:

[   ]

Examples: doctor, build houses

Search ➔

"I'm not really sure."

👤

Tell us what you
like to do.

Answer questions about the type of work you might enjoy. We'll suggest careers that match your interests and training.

Start ➔

Another approach is to provide you with the necessary tools to find the best fit for your personality. This will also help in understanding the natural strengths and weaknesses that your personality has, and how they can be leveraged in your new career. The *__Myers Briggs Assessment__* is the tool we are going to use. Based on the amount of resources that are available for you, via the internet, at no cost, take the free online test. At the completion of this test, you will be given a four-letter code that is explained in the online job search steps to success website with some career and personality type information that will start your discovery process to match your personality with a career that will fulfill your expectations and goals that you have personally.

The Millstone Of Turning Your Passion Into Your Profession

Get To Know Yourself

The first step to turning your passion into your profession is to find out about you. We are going to use the Myers Briggs Personality types.

This test is available for free on the Internet; you can find it by searching for "free Myers Briggs test."
An example website is http://www.humanmetrics.com/cgi-win/jtypes2.asp

During this test you will be tested in four areas evaluated in two possible outcomes, which makes a total of one out of sixteen personality types.

The first area tested is where you are determined to be either Extraverted or Introverted:

E -- Extraverted: turned toward the outer world, of people and things. An extravert, or extraverted type, is one whose dominant function is focused in an external direction. Extraverts are inclined to express themselves using their primary function directly.

I -- Introverted: turned toward the inner world of symbols, ideals, and forms. An introvert, or introverted type, is one whose dominant function is inwardly focused. Introverts are inclined to express themselves, using their primary function, indirectly, through inference and nuance.

The second area tested is where you are determined to be either perceiving or sensing

N -- iNtuition: "Unconscious perceiving." Intuition involves the recognition of patterns, the perception of the abstract; it is a visionary sense. Extraverted intuition perceives the patterns and possibilities of life. Introverted intuition compares the "rightness" of real-world circumstances with that which is ideal. In Jung's typology, intuition is an irrational function. Intuition's opposite function is Sensing.

S -- Sensing: physiological perception; perceiving with the five natural senses. Extraverted sensors are attuned to the world of sights, sounds, smells, touches and tastes. Introverted sensors are most aware of how those perceptions compare with their ideal internal standards. In Jung's typology, sensing is an irrational function. Sensing's opposite is iNtuition.

The third area tested is where you are determined to be either thinking of feeling

T -- Thinking: Making decisions impersonally. In Jung's typology, thinking is a rational function. Thinking's opposite is Feeling.

F -- Feeling: Making decisions from a personal perspective. In Jung's typology, feeling is a rational function. Feeling's opposite is Thinking.

7

The Fourth area tested is where you are determined to be either P or J which can be interpreted different ways as shown below.

P stands for Perceiving, J for Judging. What they really represent is, again, complex. For the E (extraverted) types, its simple enough - P means that the dominant function is a Perceiving function (iNtuition or Sensing); J means the dominant function is a deciding or Judging function.
For Introverts, it's just the opposite. P means that the extraverted function is a Perceiving (data-collecting, or irrational) function, but since the dominant function is introverted (by definition for Introverts), the I _ _ P types' first functions are Judging (deciding or rational) functions.

There are 16 different combinations that are possible which each have different personality types that we are going to explore not only to find yours but also understand other think and act differently with different priorities which may be natural to them but unnatural to you. This information is also useful when you are in a situation where you have to interact with another personality type, with this information you may see how or why they do the things they do. They are listed below.

ISTJ - The Duty Fulfillers	ENTJ - The Executives
ESTJ - The Guardians	INTJ - The Scientists
ISFJ - The Nurturers	ENTP - The Visionaries
ESFJ - The Caregivers	INTP - The Thinkers
ISTP - The Mechanics	ENFJ - The Givers
ESTP - The Doers	INFJ - The Protectors
ESFP - The Performers	ENFP - The Inspirers
ISFP - The Artists	INFP - The Idealists

__Careers for ISTJ Personality Types__

"Realism, Duty, Responsibility" that is ISTJ personality and just a few of the characteristics comprising the list of personality traits your personality type naturally uses in career choice.

ISTJs are quiet, serious, responsible, sensible, patient, conservative, loyal and steadfast maintainers of society's time-honored traditions and institutions. This "Rock of Gibraltar" type needs to be needed and readily takes on a parental role, in their working relationships, as well as with friends and family. They often settle in occupations in law enforcement or government, teaching, banking and finance, religious service or administration, or business. They are ideally suited to positions in bureaucratic organizations, and they naturally adapt to playing the roles assigned to them--whether as leaders or followers. ISTJs function well in jobs requiring accurate record keeping of facts-and-figures. They are the enforcers of law, policy, procedure, schedules, and principles, and they exert a stabilizing effect on society. Hard work, honesty, politeness, timeliness and faithfulness to family, friends and country are foremost among the ISTJ's honored values. They tend to resist unnecessary change in all aspects of their lives, and they see most innovation as disruptive.

Introverted with Sensing, Thinking and Judging your career personality profile would include the following natural tendencies:

- Depth of concentration
- Reliance upon facts
- Use of logic and analysis
- Ability to organize
- Grounded in reality
- Naturally dependable
- Decisiveness
- Follow through

There are more natural traits making up yourself personality profile but those above indicate a natural ability for careers in management, particularly in the areas of government, public service, and private business.

The ISTJ personality type will also gravitate to careers requiring an organized approach to information, people, or things.

Your normally calm, quiet, patient composure will bring stability to most work settings. Your demeanor will draw trust from others that naturally enhance any leader. While it is fair and accurate to say that all the 16 personality types can lead, your type is quite natural at leadership/supervision.

Possible Career Paths for the ISTJ:

Accountant
Actuary
Architect
Archivist
Association Manager/Advisor
Auditor
Bank Examiner
Biology Specimen Technician
Biomedical Technologist
Chief Information Officer
Computer Engineer
Computer Programmer/Specialist
Construction Manager
Coroner
Corrections Officer
Cost Estimator
Court Clerk
Credit Analyst
Criminalist Or Ballistics Expert
Database Administrator
Dentist
EEG Technologist/Technician
Efficiency Expert/Analyst
Environmental Compliance Inspector
Environmental Science Technician
Estate Planner
Exercise Physiologist
Fire Prevention And Protection Specialist
Geologist
Government Employee
Hardware Engineer
Hardware/Software Tester
Immigration And Customs Inspector
Industrial Safety And Health Engineer
Insurance Claims Examiner/Underwriter
Investment Securities Officer
IRS Agent
Judge
Lab Technologist

Landscape Architect
Law Researcher
Librarian
Manager/Supervisor
Mechanical/Industrial/Electrical Engineer
Medical Records Technician
Medical Researcher
Meteorologist
Nursing Administrator
Office Manager
Optometrist
Orthodontist
Paralegal/Legal Secretary
Pharmacist/Pharmacy Technician
Physician
Pilot (Commercial)
Police Officer/Detective
Probation Officer
Property Manager
(Commercial/Residential)
Public Health Officer
Purchasing Agent And Contract Specialist
Real Estate Agent
Regulatory Compliance Officer
School Principal
Sport Equipment/Merchandise Sales
Statistician
Surgeon
Surgical Technologist
Systems Analyst
Tax Preparer And Examiner
Teacher (Technical, Industrial, Math,
Physical Education)
Technical Writer
Treasurer/Controller/Chief Financial
Officer
Veterinarian
Web Editor
Word Processing Specialist

**More information can be found on the Internet by searching for "careers for ISTJ" **

ISTJ Relationships

The ISTJ's word is as good as gold, and they honor their commitments faithfully. They believe that to do otherwise would be nothing less than a breach of honor and trustworthiness. Consequently, they take their vows very seriously, and once they have said "I do", that means they are bound to the relationship until "death do us apart" or otherwise. ISTJs are driven to fulfill their responsibilities and duties and will do so with tireless effort. They will do their best to meet the obligations presented by the different relationship roles which they play during their lives, i.e., spouse, parent, offspring, etc. They may have difficulty showing warmth, but they frequently feel it in abundance, and most develop the ability to show it through sheer effort. If nothing else, the ISTJ holds the gold medal of all the personality types for Effort. They will put forth tremendous amounts of effort to accomplish goals which are important to them. If healthy relationships are among these goals, you can bet that the ISTJ will do everything that they can to foster and maintain healthy relationships.

ISTJ Strengths

- The ability to really think something over before committing, won't act impulsively
- The ability to speak up naturally, they typically won't "shrink" from a potential confrontation
- The ability to be naturally aware of organizational guiding principles and philosophies
- The ability to initially and instantly focus upon the facts of a situation, the specifics of current or past situations
- The ability to be ""really"" practical, they will work on what is and what is "right now"
- The ability to take things literally and at face value
- The ability to keep things "grounded" and based upon previous experience and reality
- The ability to naturally identify inconsistencies, deficiencies in plans and ideas
- The ability to easily engage in debate, give and take, even constructive argument/criticism
- The ability to step back and be very impersonal
- The ability to commit and stick to plans, schedules
- The ability to focus, ponder, deliberate
- The ability to finish what they begin regardless of time constraints
- The ability to organize well
- The ability to administrate

11

ISTJ Weaknesses

- May need to be asked what you think or feel
- May view meetings as naturally negative events that "cause" more work than is accomplished by having them
- Will have difficulty seeing the big picture
- May have difficulty multi-tasking without great stress
- May seem distant and unapproachable
- Sometimes insensitive to others
- Don't allocate much time toward building relationships
- Will be uncomfortable to troubled proceeding without plans
- May initially see "new" things as immediately negative

Potential Problem Areas

With any gift of strength, there is an associated weakness. Without "bad", there would be no "good." Without "difficult," there would be no "easy." We value our strengths, but we often curse and ignore our weaknesses. To grow as a person and get what we want out of life, we must not only capitalize upon our strengths, but also face our weaknesses and deal with them. That means taking a hard look at our personality type's potential problem areas.

Most of the weaker characteristics that are found in ISTJs are due to their dominant Introverted Sensing function controlling the personality to the point that all other functions are being used to defend Sensing demands, rather than for their more balanced purposes. In such cases, an ISTJ may show some or all of the following weaknesses in varying degrees:

- Excessive love of food and drink
- Lack of interest in other people, or in relating to them
- Occasional inappropriate emotional displays
- General selfish "look after oneself" tendencies
- Uses judgment to dismiss other's opinions and perspectives, before really understanding them
- May judge others rather than themselves
- May look at external ideas and people with the primary purpose of finding fault
- May become slave to their routine and "by the book" ways of doing things, to the point that any deviation is completely unacceptable
- May have difficulty communicating their thoughts and feelings to anyone

Ten Rules to Live By to Achieve ISTJ Success

1. *Feed Your Strengths!* Do things that allow your excellent organizational and logical abilities to flourish. Explore the worlds of business management, accounting, and medicine.

2. *Face Your Weaknesses!* See your weaknesses for what they are and seek to overcome them. Especially, strive to use your judgment against your internal store of knowledge, rather than as a means of disregarding other people's ideas.

3. *Talk Through Your Thoughts.* You need to step through your vast amount of information in order to put things into perspective. Give yourself appropriate time to do this and take advantage of discussing ideas with others. Some find that externalizing your thoughts is a valuable exercise, as is expressing your ideas clearly in writing.

4. *Take in Everything.* Don't dismiss ideas prematurely because you don't respect the person generating the ideas, or because you think you already know it all. After all, everybody has something to offer, and nobody knows everything. As Steven Covey says, "Seek first to understand, and then to be understood."

5. *Quench Your Desire to Control Others.* Remember that most people do not want to be controlled. Again, turn your controlling tendencies inwardly rather than outwardly. You can only really control yourself.

6. *Be Aware of Others.* Take time to notice where others are coming from. What is their personality type? How are they currently feeling?

7. *Be Accountable for Yourself.* Don't blame the problems in your life on other people. Look inwardly for solutions.

8. *Be Gentle in Your Expectations.* Judge yourself at least as harshly as you judge others.

9. *Assume the Best.* Don't distress yourself and others by dwelling on the dark side of everything. Just as there is a positive charge for every negative charge, there is a light side to every dark side. Remember that positive situations are created by positive attitudes, and vice versa. Expect the best, and the best will come forward.

10. *There is Nothing to Fear but Fear Itself.* Sometimes it's necessary to take a risk to initiate change. Don't be afraid to do so when that time comes. In most cases, the obstacles and burdens standing in the way of your goal are not really there--they just exist in your perspective. Change your perspective--change your life.

Careers for ESTJ Personality Types

Assertive, practical, rational, loyal, opinionated, and decisive, the ESTJ is an organized, take-charge person who brings others into line by assigning tasks and roles, giving clear-cut instructions, following up regularly to check progress and giving formal recognition to those who do as they've been told. The ESTJ usually prefers to enforce existing policies, rather than to innovate, revise or otherwise introduce unnecessary change into any system. Traditional and conservative, the ESTJ tends to apply a military model to most life situations, preferring linear channels of communication and command and eliminating any disorganization or confusion. In business, education, administration, law enforcement or the military, this type is evident as the outgoing, no-nonsense leader, gratified by the precision of smoothly functioning organizations and the power and control that come with being in charge. While others may charge that this type is sometimes short on feelings and finesse, ESTJs will tell you they express their caring by looking after others' welfare in unemotional ways.

Whether you're a young adult trying to find your place in the world, or a not-so-young adult trying to find out if you're moving along the right path, it's important to understand yourself and the personality traits which will impact your likeliness to succeed or fail at various careers. It's equally important to understand what is really important to you. When armed with an understanding of your strengths and weaknesses, and an awareness of what you truly value, you are in an excellent position to pick a career which you will find rewarding.

ESTJs generally have the following traits:

- Natural leaders - they like to be in charge
- Value security and tradition
- Loyal
- Hard-working and dependable
- Athletic and wholesome
- Have a clear set of standards and beliefs which they live by
- No patience with incompetence or inefficiency
- Excellent organizational abilities
- Enjoy creating order and structure
- Very thorough
- Will follow projects through to completion
- Straightforward and honest
- Driven to fulfill their duties

ESTJs have a lot of flexibility in the types of careers that they choose. They are good at a lot of different things, because they put forth a tremendous amount of effort towards doing things the right way. They will be happiest in leadership positions, however, because they have a natural drive to be in charge. They are best suited for jobs which require creating order and structure.

The following list of professions is built on our impressions of careers which would be especially suitable for an ESTJ. It is meant to be a starting place, rather than an exhaustive

14

list. There are no guarantees that any or all of the careers listed here would be appropriate for you, or that your best career match is among those listed.

Possible Career Paths for the ESTJ:

Accounting Internal Auditor
Administrator
Athletic Coach
Athletic Trainer
Auditor
Aviation Inspector
Bank Manager/Loan Officer
Budget Analyst
Chief Information Officer
Civil/Mechanical/Metallurgical Engineer
Clergy/Minister
Clinical Technician
Commercial Airplane Pilot
Community Health Worker
Computer Analyst
Cook
Corporate Finance Lawyer
Court Clerk
Credit Analyst/Counselor
Database Administrator/Manager
Dentist
EEG Technician
Environmental Compliance Inspector
Executive
Factory Supervisor
Funeral Director
General Contractor
Government Employee
Hospitality Manager
Industrial Engineer
Insurance Adjuster
Insurance Agent
Judge
Lawyer
Legislative Assistant
Licensing Examiner/Inspector

Logistics And Supply Manager
Management Consultant
Network Administrator
Office Manager
Paralegal
Pathologist
Pharmaceutical Sales
Pharmacist
Physician, General Medicine
Police/Probations/Corrections Officer
Primary Care Physician
Private Sector Executive
Project Manager
Property Manager, Commercial/Residential
Public Relations Specialist
Purchasing Agent
Real Estate Agent/Appraiser
Recreational Therapist
Regulatory Compliance Officer
Sales (Tangibles)
Sales Agent (Securities, Commodities)
School Administrator
School Principal
Security Guard
Social Services Worker
Sound Technician
Sports Merchandiser
Stockbroker
Teacher, Technical Trades
Technical Trainer
Telecommunications Security
Transport Coordinator
Treasurer, Controller, Chief Financial Officer
Underwriter

**More information can be found on the Internet by searching for "careers for ESTJ" **

ESTJ Relationships

ESTJs are very enthusiastic people who are driven to fulfill their obligations and duties, especially those towards their families. Their priorities generally put God first, family second, and friends third. They put forth a tremendous amount of effort to meet their obligations and duties, according to their priorities. They are dedicated and committed to their relationships, which they consider to be lifelong and unalterable. They like to be in charge and may be very controlling of their mates and children. They have high esteem for traditions and institutions and expect that their mates and children will support these as well. They have little patience and need for dealing with people who see things very differently from the ESTJ.

ESTJ Strengths

- Generally enthusiastic, upbeat, and friendly
- Stable and dependable, they can be counted on to promote security for their families
- Put forth a lot of effort to fulfill their duties and obligations
- Responsible about taking care of day-to-day practical concerns around the house
- Usually good (albeit conservative) with money
- Not personally threatened by conflict or criticism
- Interested in resolving conflict, rather than ignoring it
- Take their commitments very seriously, and seek lifelong relationships
- Able to move on after a relationship breaks up
- Able to administer discipline when necessary

ESTJ Weaknesses

- Tendency to believe that they are always right
- Tendency to need to always be in charge
- Impatient with inefficiency and sloppiness
- Not naturally in tune with what others are feeling
- Not naturally good at expressing their feelings and emotions
- May inadvertently hurt others with insensitive language
- Tendency to be materialistic and status-conscious
- Generally uncomfortable with change, and moving into new territories

Potential Problem Areas

With any gift of strength, there is an associated weakness. Without "bad", there would be no "good." Without "difficult", there would be no "easy." We value our strengths, but we often curse and ignore our weaknesses. To grow as a person and get what we want out of life, we must not only capitalize upon our strengths, but also face our weaknesses and deal with them. That means taking a hard look at our personality type's potential problem areas.

Most of the weaker characteristics that are found in ESTJs are due to Extraverted Thinking taking over the personality to the extent that other functions work only to serve Extraverted

Thinking's agenda. In such cases, an ESTJ may show some or all of the following weaknesses in varying degrees:

- May be unaware or uncaring of how they come across to others.
- May deliberately bully people into behaving a certain way (with the justification that they're enforcing a principle.)
- May quickly dismiss input from others without really considering it.
- May have difficulty communicating their thoughts and feelings to others.
- Maybe have difficulty understanding the importance of considering people's feelings and trying to meet their emotional needs.
- May hold grudges and have difficulty forgiving people.
- May have an intense and quick temper.
- May be highly controlling towards others.
- May be unable to place value on individual life.
- May be unable to see the long-term impact of their behavior.

Ten Rules to Live By to Achieve ESTJ Success

1. *Feed Your Strengths!* You have been given the great ability to create logical, ethical principles that transcend personal experience. Allow these principles to be as good as they can be by creating them with consideration for all available data.
2. *Face Your Weaknesses!* See your weaknesses for what they are and seek to overcome them. Especially, resist the tendency to judge too quickly, and remember the importance of considering other people's feelings.
3. *Talk Through the Facts or Write Them Down.* You need to step through the facts in order to define good principles to live by. Verbalizing them or putting them down on paper may be a valuable tool for you.
4. *Take in Everything.* Don't dismiss ideas prematurely because you think you already know the answer. Seek first to understand, and then to be understood.
5. *When You Get Angry, You Lose.* Your passion for your principles is admirable but becomes destructive when you fall into the "Anger Trap." Remember that Anger is destructive to personal relationships and can be extremely hurtful to others. Work through your anger before you unleash it upon others. Disagreements and disappointments can only be handled effectively in a non-personal and dispassionate manner.
6. *Be Yourself in Relationships.* Don't expect yourself to be a "touchy-feely" or "warm and fuzzy" person. Realize that your most ardent bonds start with the head, rather than the heart. You expect your actions to speak for themselves to your loved ones. This may not be enough for some. Be aware of other's emotional needs and express your genuine love and respect for them in terms that are real to YOU. Be yourself.
7. *Be Accountable for Yourself.* Don't blame the problems in your life on other people. Look inwardly for solutions. No one has more control over your life than you have.
8. *Be Humble.* Judge yourself at least as harshly as you judge others.
9. *Resist the Urge to Control Others.* You can't force others to adhere to your ways of thinking. You may think that you know what's best for others, but you really only know how they can best act according to your ideas of what is right. Just as you are

entitled to live as you see fit, so are they. Instead of judging and controlling others, focus on using your judgment to create better impartial principles.

10. ***Spend Some Time Alone.*** Encourage the development of your introverted side. You'll find many tangible benefits to becoming a better-rounded person.

Careers for ISFJ Personality Types

ISFJs are private, faithful, sensible, and sensitive. Shy, modest, and unassuming, this type needs to support and minister to others in order to feel useful. Others count on the ISFJ's steadfast caring and help--so much so that they may become irresponsibly dependent on this type's support. Martyrdom is often an occupational hazard for self-sacrificing ISFJs, who may have to struggle with inner doubts and fears before expressing their personal needs and desires. Work is life to these conservative souls, who put in long hours at the workplace, as well as at home. ISFJs volunteer their help generously, often behind the scenes. Innovation, change, and uncertainty are unnerving to these folks. They prefer a stable, organized, well regulated, scheduled life, even if someone else is to control what will happen and when. The deeply compassionate ISFJ gravitates toward traditional helping occupations: human services, the ministry, homemaking, teaching, and clerical work. They are happy handling details and routine, especially if there is a human element in the work they do.

Whether you're a young adult trying to find your place in the world, or a not-so-young adult trying to find out if you're moving along the right path, it's important to understand yourself and the personality traits which will impact your likeliness to succeed or fail at various careers. It's equally important to understand what is really important to you. When armed with an understanding of your strengths and weaknesses, and an awareness of what you truly value, you are in an excellent position to pick a career which you will find rewarding.

ISFJs generally have the following traits:

- Large, rich inner store of information which they gather about people
- Highly observant and aware of people's feelings and reactions
- Excellent memory for details which are important to them
- Very in tune with their surroundings - excellent sense of space and function
- Can be depended on to follow things through to completion
- Will work long and hard to see that jobs get done
- Stable, practical, down-to-earth - they dislike working with theory and abstract thought
- Dislike doing things which don't make sense to them
- Value security, tradition, and peaceful living
- Service-oriented: focused on what people need and want
- Kind and considerate
- Likely to put others' needs above their own
- Learn best with hands-on training
- Enjoy creating structure and order
- Take their responsibilities seriously
- Extremely uncomfortable with conflict and confrontation

ISFJs have two basic traits which help define their best career direction: 1) they are extremely interested and in tune with how other people are feeling, and 2) they enjoy creating structure and order, and are extremely good at it. Ideally, the ISFJ will choose a career in which they can use their exceptional people-observation skills to determine what people want or need, and then use their excellent organizational abilities to create a structured plan or environment for achieving what people want. Their excellent sense of space and function combined with their awareness of aesthetic quality also gives them quite special abilities in the more practical artistic endeavors, such as interior decorating and clothes design.

The following list of professions is built on our impressions of careers which would be especially suitable for an ISFJ. It is meant to be a starting place, rather than an exhaustive list. There are no guarantees that any or all of the careers listed here would be appropriate for you, or that your best career match is among those listed.

Possible Career Paths for the ISFJ:

Artist
Athletic Trainer
Bank Trust Officer
Biochemist
Biologist
Bookkeeper
Botanist
Child Life Specialist
Clerical Supervisor
Computer Operator
Computer Support Specialist
Corrections Officer
Corrective Therapist
Counselor
Curator
Customer Service Representative
Dental Hygienist/Technician
Dietitian/Nutritionist
Educational Administrator
Physician
Fashion Merchandiser
Fish And Game Warden
Franchise Owner, Retail
Funeral Director
Genealogist
Grant Coordinator
Health Care Administrator
Health Technician
Historian
Home Economist
Home Health Aide
Home Health Social Worker

Hospice Worker
Hotel/Motel Manager
Interior Decorator
Jeweler
Librarian/Archivist
Massage Therapist
Medical Equipment Salesperson
Medical Records Administrator
Medical Researcher
Medical Technologist
Merchandise Planner
Minister
Museum Research Worker
Musician
Nurse
Occupational Therapist
Optician
Orthodontist
Paralegal
Personnel Administrator
Pharmaceutical Salesperson
Pharmacist/Pharmacy Technician
Physical Therapist
Police Detective
Police Identification And Records Specialist
Probation Officer
Real Estate Agent/Broker
Religious Worker
Respiratory Therapist
Secretary
Social Worker

19

Speech Pathologist
Surgical Technologist/Technician
Tax Preparer
Teacher (K-12)
Teacher (Preschool)

Teacher (Special Education)
Title Examiner Or Abstractor
Veterinarian

**More information can be found on the Internet by searching for "careers for ISFJ" **

ISFJ Relationships

ISFJs place a great deal of importance on their personal relationships. They're generally very giving and loving people, who place the needs of others above their own. They sometimes have a problem with becoming overly emotionally needy, and with keeping their true feelings hidden from others. They take their commitments very seriously and seek lifelong relationships. ISFJs are extremely dependable and put forth a lot of energy into keeping things running smoothly. They sometimes have difficulty saying "no" when asked to do something, and therefore may be taken for granted.

ISFJ Strengths

- Warm, friendly, and affirming by nature
- Service-oriented, wanting to please others
- Good listeners
- Will put forth lots of effort to fulfill their duties and obligations
- Excellent organizational capabilities
- Good at taking care of practical matters and daily needs
- Usually good (albeit conservative) at handling money
- Take their commitments seriously, and seek lifelong relationships

ISFJ Weaknesses

- Don't pay enough attention to their own needs
- May have difficulty branching out into new territory
- Extreme dislike of conflict and criticism
- Unlikely to express their needs, which may cause pent-up frustrations to build inside
- Have difficulty leaving a bad relationship
- Have difficulty moving on after the end of a relationship

Potential Problem Areas

With any gift of strength, there is an associated weakness. The strong expression of any function can overshadow others, whilst at the same time its own associated and unexpressed inferior function can mine the unconscious mind and throw up annoying resistances and unsettling emotions. We value our strengths, but we often curse and - even more limiting to our potential development - ignore our weaknesses. To grow as a person and get what we want out of life, we must not only capitalize upon our strengths, but also face our weaknesses and deal with them. That means taking a hard look at our personality type's potential problem areas.

ISFJs are kind, steady, and responsible beings with many special gifts. I would like for the ISFJ to keep in mind some of the many positive things associated with being an ISFJ as they read some of this more negative material. Also remember that the weaknesses associated with being an ISFJ are natural to your type. Although it may be depressing to read about your type's weaknesses, please remember that we offer this information to enact positive change. We want people to grow into their own potential, and to live happy and successful lives.

Many of the weaker characteristics that are found in ISFJs are due to their dominant and Introverted Sensing function overshadowing the rest of their personality. This generally results in two notable effects: their Extraverted Feeling function is unable to balance their sharply rendered inner perceptions with a sense of human value, whilst at the same time these very perceptions often hint at strange associations and consequences which seem always to hover darkly in the background of the world

In such cases, an ISFJ may show some or all of the following weaknesses in varying degrees:

- May find difficulty expressing their feelings without fear or anger.
- May be unable to correctly judge what really is for the best
- May wrongly suspect others of having hidden motives or agendas
- May be unable to shrug off feelings impending disaster
- May be unable to acknowledge or hear anything that goes against their certainty about the "correct" or "right" way to do things
- May have a tendency to blame particular persons for disturbing or upsetting "their world" by simply being who they are
- May come across to others as cold and insensitive to anything but another's ability to fit in with and support their own judgments
- May be unnecessarily harsh or strict about appropriate social behavior
- May be oblivious to what others think about them
- May come across as rigid, inflexible, or even cold and uncaring to others, without being aware of it
- May be unable to understand verbal logic, and quickly cut off other's explanations
- May value their own certainties about the world and its problems far above others
- May be quite falsely certain of their influence upon, and understanding of others

21

- May be extremely vulnerable to tricks, con men, false hopes, religious cults, and conspiracy theories
- May react with anger or distress when someone expresses disagreement with their view of the world, or disapproval of their judgments
- May favor their judgments to the degree that they are unable to notice the pain or difficulty such judgments might cause others
- Under great stress, are likely to make outrageously harsh and uncaringly selfish survival-oriented decisions

Ten Rules to Live By to Achieve ISFJ Success

1. *Feed Your Strengths!* Let your talent for recognizing harmony and balance spill out into the world around you, show your gifts to the world. Allow yourself to take opportunities to design, reorganize and rebalance things to make your home and work environments better for yourself and others. Find work or a hobby which allows you to realize these strengths.

2. *Face Your Weaknesses!* Realize and accept that some things are never going to be how you would like them to be. Understand that other people's feelings are sometimes more important than whether they are right or wrong. Facing and dealing with discord or differences in others doesn't mean that you have to change who you are; it means that you are giving yourself opportunities to grow. By facing your weaknesses, you honor your true self and that of others.

3. *Discover the World of Others.* Don't let yourself fall into the trap of thinking you always know what is right for others. Open your heart to the possibility of understanding that their true needs are something that must be discovered through relationship, and recognition that their world might be very different, yet just as valid as your own.

4. *Don't be too hasty.* Try to let things settle before you make a judgment, allowing others to discover the best for themselves while you feel your way into their way of seeing things.

5. *Look Carefully at the World.* Remember, things are not always what they seem on the surface. You might need to look deeper to discover the truth, particularly when it seems you are sure of your first quick judgment. There are layers of meaning and truth beneath everything.

6. *Try to Let Others Take Some of the Load.* By letting others help, you are not letting things get out of control, but are validating their own need to be a part of your life. Remember, it is better to guide another to see your point of view than keeping them out of the picture.

7. *Be Accountable to Others.* Remember that they need to understand you and your needs too. Express your feelings and reasons and let them become partners to your goals.

8. *Don't Hem Yourself In.* Staying in your comfort zone is self-defeating in the end. Try to make every day one where you get out and discover a little something different about the world and others. This will broaden your horizons and bring new ideas and opportunities into focus.

9. ***Assume The Best And Seek For It.*** Don't wait for others to live up to your expectations. Every person has a goldmine of worth in them, just as every situation can be turned to some good. If you let yourself believe this, you will find yourself discovering ways to make it true for you.

10. ***When In Doubt, Ask For Help!*** Don't let your sense of self sufficiency leave you on the horns of a dilemma or lead you into disaster. If you are uncertain of something or someone then get input from others you trust.

Careers for ESFJ Personality Types

ESFJs are outgoing, sociable, practical, and organized. They pride themselves on their reflexive skills to harmonize, entertain and nurture others. Duty, personal service, manners, and social order come second-nature to this type. Warm, friendly, and naturally talented at working with others and organizing people and events, ESFJs make excellent salespeople, health care providers, teachers, homemakers, and hosts. They work well as club and committee members, and their type numbers conspicuously among volunteer, church, charitable, social, and civic organizations. Traditional, conservative, and loyal, ESFJs work hard, devoting their time and energy to family and friends. This caring type has little tolerance for those whose actions or omissions hurt others' feelings, and they may let the offender know! Although ESFJs derive personal satisfaction from helping others, they need verbal and tangible strokes of appreciation for their good work. When they do not receive the kind of recognition and reciprocation, they feel is due, ESFJs may suffer attacks of righteous indignation.

Whether you're a young adult trying to find your place in the world, or a not-so-young adult trying to find out if you're moving along the right path, it's important to understand yourself and the personality traits which will impact your likeliness to succeed or fail at various careers. It's equally important to understand what is really important to you. When armed with an understanding of your strengths and weaknesses, and an awareness of what you truly value, you are in an excellent position to pick a career which you will find rewarding.

ESFJs generally have the following traits:

- Organized
- Loyal
- Can be depended on to follow things through to completion
- Enjoy creating order, structure, and schedules
- Enjoy interacting with people
- Warm-hearted and sympathetic
- Tend to put others' needs above their own
- Very good at giving practical care
- Very cooperative, good team members
- Practical and down-to-earth
- Value peaceful living and security
- Enjoy variety, but work well with routine tasks
- Need approval from others
- Receive satisfaction from giving to others
- Live in the here and now - dislike theorizing about the future

The ESFJ has two primary traits which will help define their best career direction: 1) they are extremely organized and enjoy creating order, and 2) much of their self-satisfaction is gotten through giving and helping others. Accordingly, they will do well at tasks which involve creating or maintaining order and structure, and they will be happiest when they are serving others.

The following list of professions is built on our impressions of careers which would be especially suitable for an ESFJ. It is meant to be a starting place, rather than an exhaustive list. There are no guarantees that any or all of the careers listed here would be appropriate for you, or that your best career match is among those listed.

Possible Career Paths for the ESFJ:

Accountant
Actor
Aerobics Instructor
Athletic Coach
Bilingual Education Teacher
Bookkeeper
Caterer
Chemist
Childcare Center Director
Child Life Specialist
Child Provider
Child Welfare Counselor
Chiropractor
Clergy—Minister/Priest/Rabbi
Community Welfare Worker
Corrective Therapist
Cosmetologist/Hairdresser
Counselor
Court Clerk
Court Reporter
Credit Counselor
Customer Relations Manager (Technology)
Customer Service Manager/Representative
Dentist/Dental Hygienist
Dialysis Technician
Dietitian/Nutritionist
Director Of Religious Education
Eco-Tourism Specialist
Employee Assistance Counselor
Exercise Physiologist
Family Physician
Flight Attendant
Food Service Manager
Fund-Raiser
Funeral Home Director
Genealogist
Health Care Administrator
Health Club Manager
Home Health Social Worker/Aide
Hospice Worker
Hotel/Motel Manager
Insurance Agent

Land Leasing And Development Specialist
Law Clerk
Legislative Assistant
Licensed Practical Nurse (LPN)
Loan Officer And Counselor
Lodging Owner/Innkeeper
Management Consultant
Marketing Executive (Radio, TV, Cable)
Medical Secretary
Medical/Dental Assistant
Merchandise Planner
Nurse
Nursery And Greenhouse Manager
Nursing Instructor
Office Manager
Optometrist/Optician
Paralegal Or Legal Assistant
Personal Banker
Personal Fitness Trainer
Pharmacist/Pharmacy Technician
Physical Therapist
Police Detective
Primary Care Physician
Property Manager (Commercial/Residential)
Psychologist
Public Relations Accountant Executive
Public Relations Specialist
Radiological Technician
Real Estate Agent/Broker/Appraise
Recreational Therapist
Respiratory Therapist
Retail Owner/Operator
Sales Representative (Tangibles)
School Principal
Secretary
Social Worker
Speech Pathologist
Sports Equipment/Merchandise Sales
Student Personnel Administrator
Substance Abuse Counselor
Teacher (Elementary, Secondary, Special Education)

Translator/Interpreter

Travel Agent

Typist

Veterinarian

Wilderness Adventure Leader

**More information can be found on the Internet by searching for "careers for ESFJ" **

ESFJ Relationships

ESFJs are warm-hearted individuals who highly value their close personal relationships. They are very service-oriented, and their own happiness is closely tied into the happiness and comfort of those around them. They are valued for their genuine warm and caring natures, and their special ability to bring out the best in others. They usually do not handle conflict well and may tend to be very controlling or manipulative. Relationships are central to their lives, and they put forth a great amount of energy into developing and maintaining their close interpersonal relationships. They expect the same from others.

ESFJ Strengths

- Put forth a lot of effort to fulfill their duties and obligations
- Warm, friendly, and affirming by nature
- Service-oriented, they want to please others
- Take their commitments very seriously, and seek lifelong relationships
- Responsible and practical, they can be counted to take care of day-to-day necessities
- Generally, upbeat, and popular, people are drawn towards them
- Generally, very good money managers
- Traditionally minded and family-oriented, they will make family celebrations and traditions special events

ESFJ Weaknesses

- Generally uncomfortable with change, and moving into new territories
- Extreme dislike of conflict and criticism
- Need a lot of positive affirmation to feel good about themselves
- May be overly status-conscious, and interested in how others see them
- Have very difficult time accepting the end of a relationship, and are likely to take the blame for the failure onto their own shoulders
- Have difficulty accepting negative things about people close to them
- Don't pay enough attention to their own needs, and may be self-sacrificing
- May tend to use guilt manipulation as a way to get what they want

Potential Problem Areas

With any gift of strength, there is an associated weakness. The strong expression of any function can overshadow others, whilst at the same time its own associated and unexpressed inferior function can mine the unconscious mind and throw up annoying resistances and unsettling emotions. We value our strengths, but we often curse and - even more limiting to our potential development - ignore our weaknesses. To grow as a person and get what we want out of life, we must not only capitalize upon our strengths, but also face our weaknesses and deal with them. That means taking a hard look at our personality type's potential problem areas.

ESFJs are kind, steady, and responsible beings with many special gifts. I would like the ESFJ to keep in mind their many positive traits as they read on and remember that the weaknesses associated with being an ESFJ are natural to your type. Although it can be depressing to read about your type's weaknesses, please remember that we offer this information to enact positive change. We want people to grow into their own potential, and to live happy and successful lives.

Many of the ESFJ's weaker characteristics arise because their dominant and Extraverted Feeling function can overshadow the rest of their personality. This generally results in two notable effects. With their Introverted Sensing function unable to provide sufficient balance to their sharply defined feeling judgements, they often miss the relativities and contingencies of the real world. This very often leads them into conflict with those who believe a situation needs to be properly analysed before its realities can be seen and acted upon. Secondly, with their sense of the world controlled by feelings alone, the narrowly defined ESFJ will nearly always find themselves at odds with any view of the world that does not see their own clearly held judgements to be primary, or which does not accord them the "feeling toned" responses they expect. This can produce a range of effects, every one of which ends in conflict for the ESFJ, either with others or with their own feelings.

Without a sound appreciation of the concrete world, an ESFJ may show some or all of the following weaknesses in varying degrees:

- May be unable to correctly judge what really is for the best
- May become spiteful and extremely intractable in the face of clear logical reasoning.
- May be unable to shrug off feelings that others are not "good people."
- May be unable to acknowledge anything that goes against their certainty about the "correct" or "right" way to do things
- May attribute their own problems to arbitrary and unprovable notions about the way people "ought" to behave.
- May be at a loss when confronted with situations that require basic technical expertise or clear thinking.
- May be oblivious to all but their own viewpoint, valuing their own certainties to the exclusion of others.
- May be unable to understand verbal logic, and quickly cut off other's explanations
- May be falsely certain of the true needs and feelings of others.
- May be extremely vulnerable to superstitions, religious cults, and media manipulation.

27

- May react too quickly and too emotionally in a situation better dealt with in a more pragmatic fashion.

Ten Rules to Live By to Achieve ESFJ Success

1. *Feed Your Strengths!* Let your talent for caring and giving spill out into the world around you, show your gifts to the world. Allow yourself to take opportunities to nurture and develop situations in your home and work environments which bring value for yourself and others. Find work or a hobby which allows you to realize these strengths.

2. *Face Your Weaknesses!* Realize and accept that some things are never going to be how you would like them to be. Understand that other peoples need to deal with the world regardless of how it seems. Facing and dealing with discord or differences in others doesn't mean that you have to change who you are; it means that you are giving yourself opportunities to grow. By facing your weaknesses, you honor your true self and that of others.

3. *Discover The World Of Others.* Don't let yourself fall into the trap of thinking you always know what is right for others. Open your heart to the possibility of understanding that their true needs are something that must be discovered through a recognition that their view of the world might be very different, yet just as valid as your own.

4. *Don't Be Too Hasty.* Try to let things settle before you make a judgment, allowing others to discover the best for themselves while you try to see all the variables and contingencies in a situation.

5. *Look Carefully At The World.* Remember, things are not always what they seem on the surface. You might need to look deeper to discover the truth, particularly when it seems you are sure of your first quick judgment. There are layers of meaning and truth beneath everything.

6. *Try To Let Others Take Some Of The Load.* By letting others make their own judgments, you are not letting things get out of control, but are validating their own need to be a part of your life. Remember, it is better to guide another to see your point of view than keeping them out of the picture.

7. *Be Accountable To Others.* Remember that they need to understand you and your needs too. Express your doubts and difficulties as well as your reasons and let them become partners to your goals.

8. *Don't Hem Yourself In.* Staying in your comfort zone is self-defeating in the end. Try to make every day one where you get out and discover a little something different about the world and others. This will broaden your horizons and bring new ideas and opportunities into focus.

9. *Assume The Best And Seek For It.* Don't wait for others to live up to your expectations. Every person has a goldmine of worth in them, just as every situation can be turned to some good. If you let yourself believe this, you will find yourself discovering ways to make it true for you.

10. *When In Doubt, Ask For Help!* Don't let your fears leave you on the horns of a dilemma or lead you into disaster. If you are uncertain of something or someone then get input from others who have greater experience in dealing with this difficulty.

Careers for ISTP Personality Types

ISTPs are factual, sensible, logical, and reflective. They enjoy activity, independence and solitude and may work happily and productively for 20 hours at a stretch. Curious, practical, and often mechanically adept, many excellent craftsmen and production artists are ISTPs, as are professionals in electronics, engineering and mechanics and stars in individual athletic competition and team sports. ISTPs are masterful at analyzing complex systems and introducing change to improve productivity and efficiency. This type is noted for working out easier ways to get things done and are often a great asset, but also a potential liability if the ISTP side-steps regulations, codes, and laws. In business and finance, ISTPs often rise to the top because they combine a no-nonsense facts-and-figures approach with a "why not try it?" openness to strategy. They tend to be objective, competitive, and coolly rational in most life pursuits. More feeling types may perceive the ISTP's approach to personal relationships as detached, conditional, and utilitarian, but ISTPs retort that their behavior is merely unemotional.

Whether you're a young adult trying to find your place in the world, or a not-so-young adult trying to find out if you're moving along the right path, it's important to understand yourself and the personality traits which will impact your likeliness to succeed or fail at various careers. It's equally important to understand what is really important to you. When armed with an understanding of your strengths and weaknesses, and an awareness of what you truly value, you are in an excellent position to pick a career which you will find rewarding.

ISTPs generally have the following traits:

- Interested in how and why things work
- Do not function well in regimented, structured environments; they will either feel stifled or become intensely bored
- Constantly gather facts about their environment and store them away
- Have an excellent ability to apply logic and reason to their immense store of facts to solve problems or discover how things work
- Learn best "hands-on"
- Usually able to master theory and abstract thinking, but don't particularly like dealing with it unless they see a practical application
- Action-oriented "doers"
- Focused on living in the present, rather than the future
- Love variety and new experiences
- Highly practical and realistic
- Excellent "trouble-shooters", able to quickly find solutions to a wide variety of practical problems
- Results-oriented; they like to see immediate results for their efforts
- Usually laid-back and easy-going with people
- Risk-takers who thrive on action
- Independent and determined - usually dislike committing themselves
- Usually quite self-confident

The ISTP is fortunate because they have the abilities to be good at many different kinds of tasks. Their introverted and thinking preferences give them the ability to concentrate and work through problems which leaves many doors open to them. However, to be happiest, the ISTP needs to lead a lifestyle which offers a great deal of autonomy and does not include much external enforcement of structure. ISTPs will do best working for themselves or working in very flexible environments. Their natural interests lie towards applying their excellent reasoning skills against known facts and data to discover underlying structure, or solutions to practical questions.

The following list of professions is built on our impressions of careers which would be especially suitable for an ISTP. It is meant to be a starting place, rather than an exhaustive list. There are no guarantees that any or all of the careers listed here would be appropriate for you, or that your best career match is among those listed.

Possible Career Paths for the ISTP:

Airplane Dispatcher/Air Traffic Controller
Animal Trainer
Audiovisual Specialist
Automotive Products Retailer
Banker
Carpenter
Coach/Trainer
Commercial Artist
Computer Engineer
Computer Programmer
Computer Repair Person
Corporate Executive
Criminal Investigator
Criminalist Or Ballistics Expert
Data Processing Equipment Repairer
Dental Assistant/Hygienist
Electronics Specialist
Emergency Medical Technician (EMT)
Emergency Room Physician
Engineer (Electrical, Mechanical, Civil)
Entrepreneur
Exercise Physiologist
Firefighter
Forester
Forensic Pathologist
Geologist
Home Network Installer/Troubleshooter
Information Services Specialists/Developers
Insurance Adjuster/ Appraiser/Examiner
Intelligence Agent (FBI, CIA, Secret Service)
Landscape Architect

Lawyer/Judge
Legal Secretary
Logistics And Supply Manager/Manufacturer
Management Consultant (Business Operations)
Marine Biologist
Marshal
Mechanic
Medical Technician
Military Officer
Model And Mold Maker
Musical Instrument Maker
Network Integration Specialist (Telecommunications)
Office Manager
Optometrist
Paralegal
Park Naturalist
Pharmaceutical Salesperson
Photographer
Physical Therapist
Pilot/Driver/Locomotive Engineer
Police/Corrections Officer
Private Investigator/Detective
Product Safety Engineer
Purchasing Agent/Buyer
Quality Assurance Technician
Respiratory Therapist
Securities Analyst
Sketch Artist
Software Engineer
Sports Equipment/Merchandise Sales

30

Stockbroker
Studio, Stage, And Special Effects
Specialist
Surgical Technician
Surveyor
Systems Analyst

Systems Support Operator/Installer
Technical Trainer (One-On-One)
Telecommunications Specialist
Television Camera Operator
Transport Coordinator
Weapons Operator

More information can be found on the Internet by searching for "careers for ISTP**" **

ISTP Relationships

ISTPs are generally extremely capable individuals who are good at most things which interest them. They are usually bright, interesting, and exciting individuals with a lot to offer. They live almost entirely in the present moment, and usually do not make commitments beyond the immediate foreseeable future. An ISTP probably coined the phrase "nothing is unconditional." They strongly prefer to take things one day at a time, rather than make long-term commitments. If a relationship interests them and satisfies their needs, the ISTP will do their part on a daily basis to keep the relationship strong and healthy. If they lose interest in a relationship, their natural tendency will be to move on.

ISTP Strengths

- Good listeners
- Usually, self-confident
- Generally optimistic and fun to be with
- Practical and realistic, they handle daily concerns
- Are not threatened by conflict or criticism
- Able to leave a relationship with relative ease once it is over
- Able to administer punishment, although they're not interested in doing so
- Likely to respect other's needs for space and privacy

ISTP Weaknesses

- Living entirely in the present, they have difficulty with long-term commitments
- Not naturally good at expressing feelings and emotions
- Not tuned in to what others are feeling, they may be insensitive at times
- Tendency to be overly private and hold back part of themselves
- Need a lot of personal space, which they don't like to have invaded
- They thrive on action and excitement, and may stir things up to create it

Potential Problem Areas

With any gift of strength, there is an associated weakness. Without "bad", there would be no "good." Without "difficult", there would be no "easy." We value our strengths, but we often curse and ignore our weaknesses. To grow as a person and get what we want out of life, we must not only capitalize upon our strengths, but also face our weaknesses and deal with them. That means taking a hard look at our personality type's potential problem areas.

Most of the weaker characteristics that are found in ISTPs are due to their dominant function of Introverted Thinking overtaking the personality to the point that all of the other functions exist merely to serve the purposes of Introverted Thinking. In such cases, an ISTP may show some or all of the following weaknesses in varying degrees:

- The ISTP gets "stuck in a rut" and only does those things that are known and comfortable to the ISTP.
- The ISTP resists and rejects anything that doesn't support their own experiential understanding of the world. If there is a conflict between their own way of life and something that they encounter, they don't perceive that "something" in an objective sense. Rather, they reject it to avoid conflict and to preserve the sanctity of their inner world.
- They choose to surround themselves with people who support their own way of life and reject people who think or live differently.
- They may become overly paranoid about social organizations and institutions trying to control them.
- They may unknowingly or uncaringly hurt people's feelings.
- They may be completely unaware of how to express their inner world to others in a meaningful way.
- They may be completely unaware of the type of communication that is often desirable and (to some degree) expected in an intimate relationship. If they are aware of the kinds of things that are appropriate to say and do to foster emotional bonding, they may be unable to appreciate the value of such actions. They may feel too vulnerable to express themselves in this fashion, and so reject the entire idea.
- If pushed beyond their comfort level to form commitments or emotional bonds, they may reject a relationship entirely.
- Under stress, they may show intense emotions that seem disproportionate to the situation.

Ten Rules to Live By to Achieve ISTP Success

1. *Feed Your Strengths!* Realize your gift at mastering your physical environment and give yourself plenty of opportunities to exercise your abilities. Ride, play, paint, work it. Much of your sense of well-being will come from these experiences.

2. *Face Your Weaknesses!* Face your fear of the unknown and get yourself into new situations. Experience new activities and people with new perspectives. Don't isolate yourself into a narrow and lonely existence.

3. *Talk About Your Thoughts.* Discussing your ideas and perceptions with others will help you to develop your Extraverted Sensing, and thus your understanding of the world. How well you use your auxiliary function is very important to your overall health and happiness.

4. *Don't Be Afraid To Love.* That's just your old inferior function trying to convince you that you're unloved and unlovable. It's not true. Just because you're not sure what to do with yourself doesn't mean that you can't learn! Go on... jump in. The water's warm.

5. *Respect Your Need For Action.* Understand that you need to be actively working with your environment to be "in the groove" with life. Don't chastise yourself for not being the sort to sit around and read a book or watch a movie. Choose a partner and companions who value active lifestyles.

6. *Recognize Social Principles.* Realize that our society functions around some basic social principles, and that our society would fail unless those principles are recognized and upheld. In a democracy, people vote. At a red stoplight, people stop. If people stopped voting because it wasn't important to their own way of life, who would be in power? If people stopped stopping at red stop lights because it didn't fit into their way of life, how could we drive safely? Your priorities and beliefs are important, but you must recognize that the external world's agenda is also important. Don't dismiss the importance of principles that don't affect your life directly.

7. *It's OK To Get Out Of Your Comfort Zone.* Understand that the only way to grow is to get outside of your comfort zone. If you're uncomfortable with an idea or situation because you're not sure how to act, that's good! That's an opportunity for growth.

8. *Identify And Express Your Feelings.* You may have a hard time figuring out exactly how you feel about someone that you're involved with. It's important that you do figure this out. Don't lead someone on with your ambivalence. If you determine that you value the person, tell them so every time you think of it. This is the best way to make them feel secure in your affections, and so to promote a long-lasting relationship.

9. *Be Aware Of Others.* Try to really identify where people are coming from. Their ideas, thoughts and priorities are different from yours. They have something to offer you. Try to identify their personality types.

10. *Assume The Best.* Don't distress yourself with fear and dark imaginings. Expect the best, and the best will come.

Careers for ESTP Personality Types

ESTPs are outgoing practical thinkers--masters of experience, observation, and the analysis of cause-effect relationships, free from the biasing influence of theory, tradition, or emotion. Action is the ESTP's middle name. This type thrives on it and creates it when life gets too boring. Resourceful troubleshooters, dynamic entrepreneurs, and engaging negotiators, ESTPs apply a flexible, common-sense reasoning approach to any problem they tackle planting a garden, fixing a car, settling a dispute, or reorganizing a multibillion-dollar corporation. Just don't try to sell this type on fantasies and abstract ideas! Spontaneous, competitive, and generous, ESTPs turn work into play, whenever possible, and apply the model of an athletic team to all their relationships. Teamwork matters to the ESTP. Although they can be charming, clever, and seductively open, rarely do ESTPs merit description as deeply feeling people. When life becomes too complex with unwanted obligations and personal entanglements, count on the ESTP to escape from the situation.

Whether you're a young adult trying to find your place in the world, or a not-so-young adult trying to find out if you're moving along the right path, it's important to understand yourself and the personality traits which will impact your likeliness to succeed or fail at various careers. It's equally important to understand what is really important to you. When armed with an understanding of your strengths and weaknesses, and an awareness of what you truly value, you are in an excellent position to pick a career which you will find rewarding. ESTPs generally have the following traits:

- Action-oriented
- Live in the present moment
- Dislike abstract theory without practical application
- Like to see immediate results for their efforts
- Fast paced and energetic
- Flexible and adaptable
- Resourceful
- Seldom work from a plan - make things up as they go
- Fun to be around
- Highly observant
- Excellent memory for details
- Excellent people skills
- Good-natured
- Excellent ability to see an immediate problem and quickly devise a solution
- Attracted to adventure and risk
- May be flashy or showy
- Like initiating things - not necessarily following them through to completion

ESTPs have some advantageous traits which are unique to their personality type. Their skills of observation make them extremely good at correctly analyzing and assessing other peoples' motives or perspectives. Their people skills allow them to use this knowledge to their advantage while interacting with people. For this reason, ESTPs are excellent salespeople. They also have a special ability to react quickly and effectively to an immediate need, such as in an emergency or crisis situation. This is a valuable skill in many different professions, perhaps most notably in action-oriented professions, such as police work. ESTPs enjoy new experiences and dealing with people, and dislike being confined in structured or regimented environments. They also want to see an immediate result for their actions, and don't like dealing with a lot of high-level theory where that won't be the case. For these reasons, they should choose careers which involve a lot of interaction with people, and do not require performing a lot of routine, detailed tasks.

The following list of professions is built on our impressions of careers which would be especially suitable for an ESTP. It is meant to be a starting place, rather than an exhaustive list. There are no guarantees that any or all of the careers listed here would be appropriate for you, or that your best career match is among those listed.

Possible Career Paths for the ESTP:

Actor/Performer
Air Traffic Controller
Artist
Audiovisual Specialist
Auditor
Banker
Budget Analyst
Car Sales
Chef
Chiropractor
Civil Engineer
Coach
Computer Programmer
Construction/Building Inspector
Corrections Officer
Criminalist Or Ballistics Expert
Dancer
Detective
Developer Of Electronic Games
Eco-Tourism Specialist
Electrical Engineer/Electronics Specialist
Emergency Medical Technician (EMT)
Entertainment Agent
Entrepreneur
Exercise Physiologist/Sports Medicine
Financial Advisor
Fitness Instructor/Trainer
Flight Engineer/Instructor
Forester
Franchise Owner
Industrial/Mechanical Engineer
Insurance Adjuster/Agent/Broker
Insurance Fraud Investigator
Intelligence Specialist

Internet Marketer
Investigator
Investor
Laboratory Technologist
Land Developer
Landscape Architect
Management Consultant
Marine Biologist
Marketing Personnel
Medical Technician
Musician
Network Integration Specialist
(Telecommunications)
News Reporter
Paramedic
Park Naturalist
Pharmacist
Photographer
Pilot
Police Officer
Probation Officer
Product Safety Engineer
Professional Athlete
Promoter
Property Manager
(Residential/Commercial)
Radio/TV Talk Show Host
Real Estate Agent
Respiratory Therapist
Retail Sales
Soil Conservationist
Sports Merchandise Sales
Sportscaster
Stockbroker

Studio, Stage, And Special Effects	Technical Trainer (Classroom Setting)
Technician	Television Camera Operator
Surveyor	Tour Guide/Agent
Systems Support Operator/Installer	Wholesaler
Teacher (Industrial, Technical, Trade)	Wilderness Adventure Leader

**More information can be found on the Internet by searching for "careers for ESTP" **

ESTP Relationships

ESTPs are gregarious and fun-loving individuals who want to make the most of every moment. They love action, and always seem to be doing something. This enthusiasm is carried over to their personal relationships, which they approach with the desire to make the most of their relationships on a daily basis. They tend to get bored easily and may be prone to switching relationships frequently unless they find an outlet for their boredom elsewhere. They approach life on a day-by-day basis, so long-term commitments are not naturally comfortable for the ESTP. They may feel tremendously committed, but they want to take their commitments day-by-day.

ESTP Strengths

- Can be quite charming
- Witty, clever, and popular
- Earthy and sensual
- Not personally threatened by conflict or criticism
- Excellent and clear-headed dealing with emergency situations
- Enthusiastic and fun-loving, they try to make everything enjoyable
- As "big kids" themselves, they're eager, willing, and able to spend time with their kids
- Likely to enjoy lavishing their loved ones with big gifts (both a strength and a weakness)

ESTP Weaknesses

- Not naturally in tune with what others are feeling
- Not naturally good at expressing feelings and emotions
- May inadvertently hurt others with insensitive language
- May be very good with money, but highly risky with it as well
- Living in the present, they're not usually good long-range planners
- May fall into the habit of ignoring conflict, rather than solving it
- Don't naturally make lifelong commitments - they take things one day at a time
- Prone to get bored easily
- More likely than other type to leave relationships quickly when they get bored
- Likely to enjoy lavishing their loved ones with big gifts (both a strength and a weakness)

Potential Problem Areas

With any gift of strength, there is an associated weakness. Without "bad", there would be no "good." Without "difficult", there would be no "easy." We value our strengths, but we often curse or simply ignore our weaknesses. To grow as a person and get what we want out of life, we must certainly exploit our strengths, but we must also face our weaknesses and deal with them. That means taking a hard look at the potential problem areas in our personality type.

It is important to realize that type weaknesses are just the blind spots behind our stronger character traits, and that the more undesirable characteristics specific to a type are usually limited to those people whose type is heavily expressed, and then only if circumstances have combined to narrow or circumvent that person's natural development. So, in reading what follows, it is worth remembering that, in describing these typical tendencies and the negative patterns of behavior which can flow from them, we are building an understanding for positive development. Every person is differently made, and we must always remember that these so called "weaknesses" are the unavoidable, understandable, and natural characteristics of our type.

Most of the weaker characteristics found in ESTPs result from Extraverted Sensing dominating their personality and co-opting the usefulness of their other functions, whilst some other difficulties stem directly from the ESTP's inability to use their less adapted functions of Extraverted Feeling and Introverted Intuition. Either singly or in combination, these ESTP traits cause most or all of the following weaknesses in varying degrees:

- Can become morose or even antagonistic in situations offering little promise of advantage or the possibility to "do something."
- May be manipulative, taking advantage of other people's weaknesses for their own gain.
- May be unwilling or unable to plan anything in advance themselves, or to follow other's careful plans.
- Can be overconfident of their own cunning or ability, ignoring problems which eventually catch up with them on their blind side.
- May find it difficult or be actually unwilling to follow through where an ongoing commitment is expected.
- In relationship situations may be overbearing, demanding and/or uncaring of the feelings of their partner.
- When alone or in reduced circumstances may be subject to dark or morbid feelings about themselves.
- May be unable to maintain employment for any length of time, losing credibility with potential employers or clients by job hopping.
- May become so engrossed in challenging activities that they lose all sense of proportion, neglecting themselves and their relationships.
- Without challenges of their own, may become focused on the behavior of others, particularly that of family or employees, insisting that they live up to what the ESTP sees as the proper code or level of accomplishment.

Ten Rules to Live By to Achieve ESTP Success

1. *Feed Your Strengths!* Give yourself every opportunity to show your innate skills. If you are not in a relationship or a job which allows this to happen, it might be time to discover ways to change this. Remember, your strengths derive from being able to deal with the world, with situations where getting things done, where opportunities to surmount difficulty exist.

2. *Face Your Weaknesses.* Try to be straight up with yourself. You have limitations others find as strengths. So what? You don't have to hide behind a curtain of fear just because you have difficulty with feelings or sorting out your inner perceptions. Allow yourself to be who you are and at the same time let others help you be more honest with your limitations.

3. *Talk About Your Thoughts.* Discussing your ideas and perceptions with others will help you to develop your separate, inner reality, make you a "real" person to them even without all that external activity. How well you use your auxiliary function is very important to your overall health and happiness.

4. *Don't Be Afraid To Show Emotion.* Your inferior functions want you to be still a child inside, and that makes you run, that makes you want to prove yourself even more. You don't have to prove anything to anyone in this regard. Everyone feel emotion and everyone is a little child inside. Find those people whose eyes tell you that you are not alone and let them hear your child's voice.

5. *Respect Your Need for Action.* Understand that you need to be actively working with your environment to be "in the groove" with life. Don't chastise yourself for not being the sort to sit around and read a book or watch a movie. Choose a partner and companions who value active lifestyles but remember to allow yourself time out to consider how their input into your life will change it. Don't just follow your nose – life is not an endless party or expedition.

6. *Recognize The Differences In Others.* Realize that everyone is different, not just a little different, but very different. Everyone has their place and value. You need to notice those values and places, places where you cannot easily fit. You can learn from these people, for they have gifts you can use, gifts they offer simply by being who they are. Try figuring out their psychological type for yourself and notice how certain types can lift you out of negative feelings just by being who they are

7. *It's OK To Get Out Of Your Comfort Zone.* Understand that the only way to grow is to get outside of your comfort zone. If you're uncomfortable with an idea or situation because you're not sure how to act, that's good! That's an opportunity for growth.

8. *Identify and Express Your Feelings.* You may have a hard time figuring out exactly how you feel about someone that you're involved with. It's important that you do figure this out. Don't lead someone on with your ambivalence. If you determine that you value the person, tell them so every time you think of it. This is the best way to make them feel secure in your affections, and so to promote a long-lasting relationship.

9. *Be Aware That You Can Fail, And That It Is OK.* Not every mountain can be climbed, not every customer will be satisfied, no matter how hard you try or no matter what tricks you bring to bear. Getting beaten is an opportunity to reflect upon what is important, what really matters in life. Next time you will take up a challenge more worthy of your skills, and more valuable to others. You can be a champion, and

it will be at your own game. Try to let it be a game of life, where everyone wins if you do.

10. *Assume The Best.* Don't distress yourself with fear and dark imaginings. Expect the best, and the best will come.

Careers for ESFP Personality Types

The ESFP is warm, outgoing, optimistic, and caring--a cheerful person who's always ready for a good time and avoids the company of dreary "doom and gloom" people who take themselves too seriously. Count on ESFPs to settle in occupations which let them be "people people"--working in sales, human services, business, nursing, crisis intervention or the performing arts. They are naturally gifted at observing human behavior and figuring out what others want. Whatever the ESFP's work choice, talking must be part of the job! To be at their best, ESFPs need to be around other people--and this type will go to great lengths to avoid solitude and isolation. ESFPs believe that life, work, and relationships should be fun and rewarding. ESFPs are unlikely to stick around when clouds darken the skies for too long at a stretch. Charming, clever, and open-minded, the witty ESFP is likely to be seen by others as a party person--so much so that this type may be ill-at-ease in business fields which expect seriousness, formality, logic, conceptual thinking, organization, and punctuality.

Whether you're a young adult trying to find your place in the world, or a not-so-young adult trying to find out if you're moving along the right path, it's important to understand yourself and the personality traits which will impact your likeliness to succeed or fail at various careers. It's equally important to understand what is really important to you. When armed with an understanding of your strengths and weaknesses, and an awareness of what you truly value, you are in an excellent position to pick a career which you will find rewarding.

ESFPs generally have the following traits:

- Live in the present moment
- Are stimulated and excited by new experiences
- Practical and realistic
- Warmly interested in people
- Know how to have a good time, and how to make things fun for others
- Independent and resourceful
- Spontaneous - seldom plan ahead
- Hate structure and routine
- Dislike theory and long written explanations
- Feel special bond with children and animals
- Strongly developed aesthetic appreciation for things
- Great people skills

ESFPs are good at many things but will not be happy unless they have a lot of contact with people, and a lot of new experiences. They should choose careers which provide them with the opportunity to use their great people skills and practical perspective, which will also provide them with enough new challenges that they will not become bored.

The following list of professions is built on our impressions of careers which would be especially suitable for an ESFP. It is meant to be a starting place, rather than an exhaustive list. There are no guarantees that any or all of the careers listed here would be appropriate for you, or that your best career match is among those listed.

Possible Career Paths for the ESFP:

Aerobics Instructor
Art Therapist
Athletic Coach
Cardiology Technologist
Cartoonist And Animator
Character Actor
Chef Or Head Cook
Childcare Provider
Child Life Specialist
Chiropractor
Costume/Wardrobe Specialist
Dental Assistant And Hygienist
Dietitian/Nutritionist
Dog Trainer
Education Software Developer
Entertainment And Sports Agent
Environmental Scientist
Exercise Physiologist
Film Producer
Floral Designer
Fund-Raiser
Geologist
Home Care Worker/Health Aide
Hospice Worker
Human Resources Diversity Manager
Insurance Agent/Broker (Health, Life)
Insurance Fraud Investigator
Interior Designer
Labor Relations Mediator
Landscape And Grounds Manager
Landscape Architect
Medical Technician
Marine Biologist
Merchandise Displayer/Planner
Musician
News Anchor
Nurse/Nursing Instructor

Occupational Therapist
Optician/Optometrist
Painter/Illustrator/Sculptor
Park Naturalist
Pediatrician
Performer (Dancer, Comedian)
Personal Fitness Trainer
Pharmacy Technician
Photographer
Physician
Podiatrist
Police/Corrections Officer
Promoter
Psychologist
Public Relations Specialist
Radio/Television Announcer
Radiological Technician
Real Estate Agent
Receptionist
Recreational Therapist
Respiratory Therapist
Retail Sales/Management
Secretary
Social Conservationist
Social Scientist
Social Worker
Special Events Coordinator
Speech And Language Pathologist
Substance Abuse Counselor
Teacher
Team Trainer
Transplant Coordinator
Travel Agent/Tour Operator
Travel Sales/Broker
Veterinarian/Veterinary Assistant
Vocational Rehabilitation Counselor
Zoologist

**More information can be found on the Internet by searching for "careers for ESFP" **

ESFP Relationships

ESFPs are fun and delightful to be with. They live for the moment and know how to make the most of each moment. They are genuinely, warmly interested in people, and love to make others happy. They're usually very kind-hearted and generous and are always going out of their way to do something nice for someone. Their affection is simple, straightforward, and honest. They dislike theory and complexities. They often resist forming relationships which require them to function on a high Intuitive or Thinking level. They prefer for things to be light and happy, although their warmth and affection runs deep. Their potential downfall is the tendency to live entirely for the present moment, and therefore to sometimes be unaware of the direction that their relationship is heading, or to be easily distracted from long-term commitments.

ESFP Strengths

- Enthusiastic and fun-loving, they make everything enjoyable
- Clever, witty, direct, and popular, people are drawn towards them
- Earthy and sensual
- Down-to-earth and practical, able to take care of daily needs
- Artistic and creative, they're likely to have attractive homes
- Flexible and diverse, they "go with the flow" extremely well
- They can leave bad relationships, although it's not easy
- Try to make the most of every moment
- Generous and warm-hearted

ESFP Weaknesses

- May be frivolous and risky with money
- Tend to be materialistic
- Extreme dislike of criticism, likely to take things extremely personally
- Likely to ignore or escape conflict situations rather than face them
- Lifelong commitments may be a struggle for them - they take things one day at a time
- Don't pay enough attention to their own needs
- Tendency to neglect their health, or even abuse their bodies
- Always excited by something new, they may change partners frequently

Potential Problem Areas

With any gift of strength, there is an associated weakness. Without "bad", there would be no "good." Without "difficult," there would be no "easy." We value our strengths, but we often curse and ignore our weaknesses. To grow as a person and get what we want out of life, we must not only capitalize upon our strengths, but also face our weaknesses and deal with them. That means taking a hard look at our personality type's potential problem areas.

ESFPs are kind and creative beings with many special gifts. I would like for the ESFP to keep in mind some of the many positive things associated with being an ESFP as they read some of this more negative material. Also remember that the weaknesses associated with being an ESFP are natural to your type. Although it may be depressing to read about your type's weaknesses, please remember that we offer this information to enact positive change. We want people to grow into their own potential, and to live happy and successful lives.

Most of the weaker characteristics that are found in ESFPs are due to their dominant Extraverted Sensing function overshadowing the rest of their personality. When this function smothers everything else, the ESFP can't use Introverted Feeling to properly judge the value and propriety of their perceptions or actions. The first ten of the following weaknesses derive in varying degrees from this problem alone, whilst the rest are due to the additional effect of the ESFPs unique make up and result from their diminished capacity to use abstract reasoning:

- May be seen by others as unnecessarily coarse in their behavior and life choices.
- May be unable to value or may ignore the preferences and needs of others.
- May perceive even the most careful and objective criticism as simply a ploy to spoil their enjoyment of life.
- May have skewed or unrealistic ideas about the feelings of others.
- May be unable to acknowledge or hear anything that would lead to second thoughts or a more careful appreciation.
- May blame their problems on the world at large, seeing themselves as frustrated heroes battling against the odds.
- May become totally self-focused and oblivious to the havoc they wreak on other people's feelings.
- May uncaringly use totally inappropriate social behavior simply to make a point.
- May be overbearing in their judgments upon the taste and dress of others.
- May come across to others as boastful and rash in their attitudes.
- May rationalize the ways of the world in the most inane or simplistic ways.
- May believe the most extraordinary things about inanimate objects and their workings.
- May feel overwhelmed with tension and stress when driven into a situation which requires deep and careful consideration.
- Under great stress, may feel the world around them is alive with dark, unseen influences.
- Another difficulty, which is not so much a problem for the ESFP but for those around them, particularly if Introverted Thinking or Intuitive types, is that even when joyful or in the midst of life, they may be perceived as coldly self-absorbed and oblivious to the feelings of others, even when the truth is quite the reverse. Should it somehow

matter, then when in the company of such people, the ESFP should take some trouble to express their feelings and value judgments.

Ten Rules to Live By to Achieve ESFP Success

1. *Feed Your Strengths!* Encourage your natural expressive abilities and hands-on talents. Nourish your appreciation of the world. Give yourself opportunities to enjoy life to the full.

2. *Face Your Weaknesses!* Realize and accept that some traits are strengths, and some are weaknesses. Facing and dealing with your weaknesses doesn't mean that you have to change who you are, it means that you want to be the best You possible. By facing your weaknesses, you are honoring your true self, rather than attacking yourself.

3. *Express Your Feelings.* Don't let worries build up inside of you. If you are troubled by doubt or fear, tell those close to you who will listen and offer counsel. Don't make the mistake of "blipping over it" or "sorting it out" some quick fix way.

4. *Listen To Everything.* Try not to accept everything at face value. Let everything soak in and listen to your feelings.

5. *Smile At Criticism.* Remember that people will not always agree with you or understand you, even if they value you greatly. Try to see disagreement and criticism as an opportunity for growth. In fact, that is exactly what it is.

6. *Be Aware Of Others.* Remember that there are 15 other personality types out there who see things differently than you see them. Try to identify other people's types. Try to understand their perspectives.

7. *Be Accountable For Yourself.* Remember that your every word and action affects those around you, so it is important for you to be fully responsible for yourself, and to the values you hold.

8. *Be Gentle In Your Expectations.* You will always be disappointed with others if you expect too much of them. Being disappointed with another person is the best way to drive them away. Treat others with the same gentleness that you would like to be treated with.

9. *Assume The Best.* Don't distress yourself by assuming the worst. Remember that a positive attitude often creates positive situations.

10. *When In Doubt, Ask Questions!* If something seems to be wrong and you can't put your finger on it, maybe someone else can. Remember, there are many ways of seeing the world, and perhaps someone else's way will reveal the truth.

Careers for ISFP Personality Types

ISFPs are quiet, practical, sensitive, and spontaneous. Somewhat shy and retiring, folks of this type are drawn to a complex array of occupations which offer some measure of solitude and also allow them to keep a finger on the pulse of life. Forestry, horticulture, farming, scuba diving, mining and construction attract some ISFPs, as do the hands-on fields of carpentry, woodworking, pottery, weaving and production art. Professional athletics, music and performance also draw a disproportionate number of this type. You'll find other ISFPs at work in a variety of human services fields, where their sensitivity and skill at observation arm them well to help others. Sensuous and earthy, many ISFPs make working or playing in the out-of-doors a high priority. The ISFP values independence strongly and tends to retreat or escape from situations which become too unpleasant, confining, or demanding. This free spirit's natural characteristics run counter to the expectations of most business organizations, so you'll rarely find this type at the top of the corporate ladder.

Whether you're a young adult trying to find your place in the world, or a not-so-young adult trying to find out if you're moving along the right path, it's important to understand yourself and the personality traits which will impact your likeliness to succeed or fail at various careers. It's equally important to understand what is really important to you. When armed with an understanding of your strengths and weaknesses, and an awareness of what you truly value, you are in an excellent position to pick a career which you will find rewarding.

ISFPs generally have the following traits:

- Keen awareness of their environment
- Live in the present moment
- Enjoy a slower pace - they like to take time to savor the present moment
- Dislike dealing with theory or abstract thought, unless they see a practical application
- Faithful and loyal to people and ideas which are important to them
- Individualistic, having no desire to lead or follow
- Take things seriously, although they frequently appear not to
- Special bond with children and animals
- Quiet and reserved, except with people they know extremely well
- Trusting, sensitive, and kind
- Service-oriented; they're driven to help others
- Extremely well-developed appreciation for aesthetic beauty
- Likely to be original and unconventional
- Learn best with hands-on training
- Hate being confined to strict schedules and regimens
- Need space and freedom to do things their own way
- Dislike mundane, routine tasks, but will perform them if necessary

The ISFP is a very special individual who needs to have a career which is more than a job. The middle of the road is not likely to be a place where they will be fulfilled and happy.

They need to have a career which is consistent with their strong core of inner values. Since they prefer to live in the current moment, and take the time to savor it, they do not do well with some of the more fast-paced corporate environments. They need a great deal of space and freedom if they are going to function in their natural realm of acute sensory awareness. If they give free reign to their natural abilities, they may find a wonderful artist within themselves. Almost every major artist in the world has been an ISFP. Since the ISFP is so acutely aware of people's feelings and reactions and is driven by their inner values to help people, the ISFP is also a natural counselor and teacher.

The following list of professions is built on our impressions of careers which would be especially suitable for an ISFP. It is meant to be a starting place, rather than an exhaustive list. There are no guarantees that any or all of the careers listed here would be appropriate for you, or that your best career match is among those listed.

Possible Career Paths for the ISFP:

Administrator
Air Traffic Controller
Archaeologist
Artist/Art Therapist
Beautician
Bookkeeper
Botanist
Cartoonist Or Animator
Chef
Clerical Supervisor
Coach (High School, College)
Computer Operator
Counselor
Crisis Hotline Operator
Dancer
Dental Hygienist/Assistant
Dietitian/Nutritionist
Exercise Physiologist
Fashion Designer
Filmmaker
Firefighter
Fish And Game Warden
Florist
Forester
Genealogist
Geologist
Horticulturist
Insurance Appraiser/Examiner
Insurance Fraud Investigator
Interior Designer
Jeweler
Landscape Architect
Legal Secretary
Librarian

Marine Biologist
Media Specialist
Medical Technician
Merchandise Planner
Museum Curator
Musician/Composer
Nurse
Occupational Therapist
Optician/Optometrist
Painter
Paralegal
Pediatrician
Personal Fitness Trainer
Pharmaceutical Researcher
Pharmacist
Physical Therapist
Physician
Pilot (Commercial)
Police/Corrections Officer
Psychologist
Public Relations Specialist
Recreation Worker
Recreational Therapist
Social Worker
Soil Conservationist
Speech Language Pathologist
Storekeeper
Surgeon
Surgical Technologist
Surveyor
Systems Analyst
Teacher (Science, Art, Music)
Teacher (Preschool)
Teacher (Special Education)

45

Television Camera Operator
Translator/Interpreter
Typist

Veterinarian
Zoologist

More information can be found on the Internet by searching for "careers for ISFP**" **

ISFP Relationships

ISFPs are warmhearted, gentle people who take their commitments seriously, and seek lifelong relationships. They are very private people, who keep their true feelings and opinions reserved or hidden from others. This may cause them to constantly defer to their mates in their intimate relationships, which may cause problems if their mates are not extremely aware of the ISFP's feelings. Some ISFPs who are in the habit of not expressing their needs and feelings find themselves in situations throughout their life where they feel overshadowed, overlooked, or even "tread upon" by others. Highly practical and cynical by nature, these feelings may cause the ISFP to become bitter, and to either give up on their relationships, or to start using their relationships for their own personal gain. Although this problem is observed sometimes in the ISFP type, it does not seem to be present in those ISFPs who consistently express their feelings to those closest to them. These ISFPs have a very positive, warm outlook on life and love, and are not as likely to find themselves in relationships where they are taken for granted or taken advantage of. ISFPs go to great lengths to please their partners. They're very loyal and supportive, with a deep capacity for love. They detest conflict and discord, and highly value being seen and understood for who they are. They need space to live their lives in their own unique way and will respect other's need for space.

ISFP Strengths

- Warm, friendly, and affirming by nature
- Usually, optimistic
- Good listeners
- Good at dealing with practical day-to-day concerns
- Flexible and laid-back, usually willing to defer to their mates
- Their love of aesthetic beauty and appreciation for function makes them likely to have attractive, functional homes
- Take their commitments seriously, and seek lifelong relationships
- Likely to value and respect other's personal space
- Likely to enjoy showing their affection through acts and deeds
- Sensuous and earthy

ISFP Weaknesses

- Not good at long-range financial (or other) planning
- Extreme dislike of conflict and criticism
- Focused on enjoying the present moment, they may appear lazy or slow-moving at times
- Need to have their own space, and dislike having it invaded
- May be slow to show their affection with words
- Tendency to hold back their thoughts and feelings, unless drawn out

46

- May become overly cynical and practical

Potential Problem Areas

With any gift of strength, there is an associated weakness. Without "bad", there would be no "good." Without "difficult", there would be no "easy." We value our strengths, but we often curse and ignore our weaknesses. To grow as a person and get what we want out of life, we must not only capitalize upon our strengths, but also face our weaknesses and deal with them. That means taking a hard look at our personality type's potential problem areas.

ISFPs are kind and creative beings with many special gifts. I would like for the ISFP to keep in mind some of the many positive things associated with being an ISFP as they read some of this more negative material. Also remember that the weaknesses associated with being an ISFP are natural to your type. Although it may be depressing to read about your type's weaknesses, please remember that we offer this information to enact positive change. We want people to grow into their own potential, and to live happy and successful lives.

Most of the weaker characteristics that are found in ISFPs are due to their dominant Feeling function overshadowing the rest of their personality. When the dominant function of Introverted Feeling overshadows everything else, the ISFP can't use Extraverted Sensing to take in information in a truly objective fashion. In such cases, an ISFP may show some or all of the following weaknesses in varying degrees:

- May be extremely sensitive to any kind of criticism
- May be unable to see the opportunities inherent to a situation
- May perceive criticism where none was intended
- May have skewed or unrealistic ideas about reality
- May be unable to acknowledge or hear anything that goes against their personal ideas and opinions
- May blame their problems on other people, seeing themselves as victims who are treated unfairly
- May have great anger, and show this anger with rash outpourings of bad temper
- May be unaware of appropriate social behavior
- May be oblivious to their personal appearance, or to appropriate dress
- May come across as eccentric, or perhaps even generally strange to others, without being aware of it
- May be unable to see or understand anyone else's point of view
- May value their own opinions and feelings far above others
- May be unaware of how their behavior affects others
- May be oblivious to other people's need
- May feel overwhelmed with tension and stress when someone expresses disagreement with the ISFP, or disapproval of the ISFP
- May develop strong judgments that are difficult to unseed against people who they perceive have been oppressive or suppressive to them
- Under great stress, may feel out of control and fearful, dwelling on the "dark side" of things

Ten Rules to Live By to Achieve ISFP Success

1. *Feed Your Strengths!* Encourage your natural artistic abilities and creativity. Nourish your spirituality. Give yourself opportunities to help the needy or underprivileged.
2. *Face Your Weaknesses!* Realize and accept that some traits are strengths, and some are weaknesses. Facing and dealing with your weaknesses doesn't mean that you have to change who you are, it means that you want to be the best You possible. By facing your weaknesses, you are honoring your true self, rather than attacking yourself.
3. *Express Your Feelings.* Don't let unexpressed emotions build up inside of you. If you have strong feelings, sort them out and express them. Don't let them build up inside you to the point where they become unmanageable!
4. *Listen To Everything.* Try not to dismiss anything immediately. Let everything soak in for a while, then apply judgment.
5. *Smile At Criticism.* Remember that people will not always agree with you or understand you, even if they value you greatly. Try to see disagreement and criticism as an opportunity for growth. In fact, that is exactly what it is.
6. *Be Aware Of Others.* Remember that there are 15 other personality types out there who see things differently than you see them. Try to identify other people's types. Try to understand their perspectives.
7. *Be Accountable For Yourself.* Remember that YOU have more control over your life than any other person has.
8. *Be Gentle In Your Expectations.* You will always be disappointed with others if you expect too much of them. Being disappointed with another person is the best way to drive them away. Treat others with the same gentleness that you would like to be treated with.
9. *Assume The Best.* Don't distress yourself by assuming the worst. Remember that a positive attitude often creates positive situations.
10. *When In Doubt, Ask Questions!* Don't assume that the lack of feedback is the same thing as negative feedback. If you need feedback and don't have any, ask for it.

Careers for ENTJ Personality Types

Outgoing, logical, and decisive, the ENTJ leads by providing conceptual structure and setting goals, rather than by detailing and enforcing procedures, codes, and regulations. This "big picture" type rises naturally to conspicuous positions of power and responsibility in all organizational settings (business, military, educational, governmental.) Disorganization, confusion, emotion, inefficiency, and illogic drive ENTJs to take charge of situations and institutions. Their intuition fuels their vision and defines their goals. They deal with the world boldly, in an assertive, analytical, objective, and organized way which inspires others to salute them and do whatever the ENTJ needs done--including all the detail work! ENTJs certainly do get things done, both at home and at work, but often at substantial cost in terms of wear and tear on the human spirit, for they may neglect the importance of the personal element in accomplishing their purpose. More than any other, this type seems to struggle between an inner drive toward creative spontaneity and the desire for order in the universe.

Whether you're a young adult trying to find your place in the world, or a not-so-young adult trying to find out if you're moving along the right path, it's important to understand yourself and the personality traits which will impact your likeliness to succeed or fail at various careers. It's equally important to understand what is really important to you. When armed with an understanding of your strengths and weaknesses, and an awareness of what you truly value, you are in an excellent position to pick a career which you will find rewarding.

ENTJs generally have the following traits:

- Driven to turn theories into plans
- Highly value knowledge
- Future-oriented
- Natural leaders
- Impatient with inefficiency and incompetence
- Want things structured and orderly
- Excellent verbal communication skills
- Dislike routine, detail-oriented tasks
- Self-confident
- Decisive

ENTJs are especially well-suited to be leaders and organization builders. They have the ability to clearly identify problems and innovative solutions for the short and long-term well-being of an organization. Having a strong desire to lead, they're not likely to be happy as followers. ENTJs like to be in charge and need to be in charge to take advantage of their special capabilities.

The following list of professions is built on our impressions of careers which would be especially suitable for an ENTJ. It is meant to be a starting place, rather than an exhaustive list. There are no guarantees that any or all of the careers listed here would be appropriate for you, or that your best career match is among those listed.

Possible Career Paths for the ENTJ:

Accountant
Actor
Advertising Account Manager
Architect
Biologist
Business Consultant
Chemical Engineer
Chief Executive Officer
College Or University Administrator
Corporate Finance Attorney
Corporate Team Trainer
Database Manager
Dentist
Economic Analyst
Economist
Educational Consultant
Employment Development Specialist
Environmental Engineer
Fine Artist
Franchise Owner
Human Resources Manager
Information Services (New Business Developer)
International Banker
International Sales And Marketing
Investment Banker
Journalist
Judge
Labor Relations Manager
Lawyer
Legislative Assistant
Life Scientist
Local Area Network (LAN) Administrator
Logistics Consultant (Manufacturing)
Management Consultant (Computer/Information Services)

Management Trainer
Marketing Executive (Radio, TV, Cable)
Marketing Manager
Media Planner/Buyer
Minister/Clergy
Mortgage Broker
Network Administrator
Network Integration Specialist (Telecommunications)
Office Manager
Pathologist
Personal Financial Planner
Personnel Manager
Photographer
Physician
Pilot
Police And Detective Supervisor
Political Consultant
Political Scientist
Program Designer
Psychiatrist
Psychologist
Real Estate Manager
Retail Manager
Robotics Network Manager
Sales Manager
School Principal
Stockbroker
Systems Administrator
Teacher (English, Science, Social Studies)
Telecommunications Security Consultant
Theater Producer
Treasurer, Controller, Chief Financial Officer
Venture Capitalist

More information can be found on the Internet by searching for "careers for ENTJ**" **

ENTJ Relationships

ENTJs put a lot of effort and enthusiasm into their relationships. Since their major quest in life is to constantly take in knowledge and turn that into something useful, the ENTJ will try to turn everything into a learning experience. Within the context of relationships, that means they will constantly seek knowledge and revise the rules and definitions of their relationships. They value their relationships highly, especially those relationships which present them with new challenges and stimulate their learning. Such exchanges promote genuine affection and satisfaction for the ENTJ. Relationships which do not offer any chances for growth or learning hold no interest to the ENTJ. As in other areas of life, the ENTJ likes to be in charge of their relationships. In conversation, they are very direct and confrontational, and can be highly critical and challenging towards others. People involved in close relationships with the ENTJ need to have a good amount of personal strength. For those who do, the ENTJ has a tremendous amount to offer.

ENTJ Strengths

- Genuinely interested in people's ideas and thoughts
- Enthusiastic and energetic
- Take their commitments very seriously
- Fair-minded and interested in doing the Right Thing
- Very good with money
- Extremely direct and straightforward
- Verbally fluent
- Enhance and encourage knowledge and self-growth in all aspects of life
- Able to leave relationships without looking back
- Able to turn conflict situations into positive lessons
- Able to take constructive criticism well
- Extremely high standards and expectations (both a strength and a weakness)
- Usually have strong affections and sentimental streaks
- Able to dole out discipline

ENTJ Weaknesses

- Their enthusiasm for verbal debates can make them appear argumentative
- Tendency to be challenging and confrontational
- Tend to get involved in "win-lose" conversations
- Tendency to have difficulty listening to others
- Tendency to be critical of opinions and attitudes which don't match their own
- Extremely high standards and expectations (both a strength and a weakness)
- Not naturally in tune with people's feelings and reactions
- May have difficulty expressing love and affection, sometimes seeming awkward or inappropriate
- Can be overpowering and intimidating to others
- Tendency to want to always be in charge, rather than sharing responsibilities
- Can be very harsh and intolerant about messiness or inefficiency
- Tendency to be controlling

- May be slow to give praise or to realize another's need for praise
- If unhappy or underdeveloped, they may be very impersonal, dictatorial, or abrasive
- Tendency to make hasty decisions
- Make explode with terrible tempers when under extreme stress

Potential Problem Areas

With any gift of strength, there is an associated weakness. Without "bad", there would be no "good." Without "difficult", there would be no "easy." We value our strengths, but we often curse and ignore our weaknesses. To grow as a person and get what we want out of life, we must not only capitalize upon our strengths, but also face our weaknesses and deal with them. That means taking a hard look at our personality type's potential problem areas.

ENTJ's are strong, right minded, and rational people. This should be kept in mind as you read some of the more negative material about ENTJ weaknesses. These weaknesses are natural. We offer this information to enact positive change, rather than as blatant criticism.

Most of the weaker characteristics in the ENTJ stem from their dominant Extraverted Thinking function overtaking their personality, stifling the natural expression, and balancing value of the other personality functions. In such cases, an ENTJ may show some or all of the following weaknesses in varying degrees:

- May be unable to understand other people's needs where these differ from their own.
- May unwisely assume their ideas are the only right ones and are therefore being fully implemented by others.
- May become childishly petulant or angered when confronted by situations which require feeling judgments.
- May become so engrossed in a plan or ambition that personal needs and the needs of others are forgotten.
- May take every decision not made in agreement with their rational beliefs as a personal rejection.
- May be easily taken in or manipulated by others via agreement with their rational attitudes.
- May become obsessed with small obstructions and difficulties to the point where the overall plan is forgotten
- May believe natural limitations are actually ailments which ought to be eradicated
- May assume others are ever plotting against them.
- May believe only their own view of the world or a situation is correct, even to the point that they make it into a kind of dogma which must be followed by those around them.

Ten Rules to Live By to Achieve ENTJ Success

1. *Feed Your Strengths!* Give yourself every opportunity to show others your appreciation of a situation and how you could see it through to a good outcome. Take charge where you can make it count.
2. *Face Your Weaknesses!* Understand you have limits too. Your careful world view is not the whole deal. How things look and feel may not concern you, but they concern many others. Try and allow such things to be and learn from them.
3. *Talk Time To Find Out How Others Really Think.* You need to drive past your thoughts with others and let their appreciations of a situation reach you at a deeper level. It will then be possible for you to take account of their needs as real-world objectives which if included in your ideas will bring greater harmony and quality to life and relationships.
4. *Take Time Out To Let The Whole Situation Speak To You.* Don't dismiss those abstract and seemingly hard to understand or bothersome aesthetic and feeling judgments coming from others or from inside yourself. Drop everything for a while, stop thinking and worrying and just relax into those ideas and let them speak to you. Perhaps they can be accommodated, perhaps something is hiding in there which offers a new way
5. *When You Get Upset, You Lose.* Your energy and rational understandings are strong assets but can be very harmful if they turn against you and leave you with nothing but emotions you cannot deal with. Remember that others cannot always be expected to fall into your ways of seeing, and when your drive to make them do so fails you will suffer feelings of resentment and even abandonment. You cannot deal with the world like this. Moderate your ideas, allow others their spaces, and you will grow.
6. *Respect Your Need For Intellectual Compatibility.* Don't expect yourself to be a "touchy-feely" or "warm-fuzzy" person. Realize that your most ardent bonds with others will start with the head, rather than the heart. Be aware of other's emotional needs and express your genuine love and respect for them in terms that are real to YOU. Be yourself.
7. *Be Accountable For Yourself.* Don't blame the problems in your life on other people. Look inwardly for solutions. No one has more control over your life than you have.
8. *Be Humble.* Judge yourself at least as harshly as you judge others.
9. *Take A Positive Approach To Differences In People.* Don't distress yourself and others by dwelling on what seem to be their limitations. They need you to guide them and you need them to see things through. Try and recognize who can perform the most ably within certain fields outside your own competence. Let the feelings of others become a strength rather than a hindrance to you.
10. *Don't Get Obsessed!* Recognize the value that personal world has to you, your friends, your family, your own inner sense of self-worth and life. Take pride in just being a good person and don't allow external situations to control you. Try to relax and let the moment belong to the best things you can find in others and yourself. Nothing out there is more important than your own happiness.

Careers for INTJ Personality Types

Independent, innovative, logical, and driven by the inner world of ideas and possibilities, the INTJ often appears to others as a quietly self-confident (and sometimes stubborn) critic of the status quo, convinced that reality can be altered, the future reshaped. Wherever there is a need for change in systems, programs, concepts, or theories, INTJs will be working behind the scenes to reorganize and revise. This type's focused attention to the personal mission may be inspiring or frankly obsessive, depending on the observer's viewpoint or the success of the enterprise. Introspective and somewhat shy, INTJs place their trust in logical analysis and intuition to guide their thoughts and decisions. More feeling types may find them chilly, and more practical types accuse them of being unrealistic, but INTJs take their cues mostly from those they recognize as intelligent. Often attracted to theoretical, analytical, and methodological areas of inquiry, INTJs succeed in a wide variety of fields, from ones heavily dependent on mathematics and science to more philosophical, literary, or applied disciplines.

Whether you're a young adult trying to find your place in the world, or a not-so-young adult trying to find out if you're moving along the right path, it's important to understand yourself and the personality traits which will impact your likeliness to succeed or fail at various careers. It's equally important to understand what is really important to you. When armed with an understanding of your strengths and weaknesses, and an awareness of what you truly value, you are in an excellent position to pick a career which you will find rewarding.

INTJs generally have the following traits:

- Able to absorb extremely complex theoretical and complex material
- Driven to create order and structure from theoretical abstractions
- Supreme strategists
- Future-oriented
- See the global, "big picture"
- Strong insights and intuitions, which they trust implicitly
- Value their own opinions over others
- Love difficult theoretical challenges
- Bored when dealing with mundane routine
- Value knowledge and efficiency
- Have no patience with inefficiency and confusion
- Have very high standards for performance, which they apply to themselves most strongly
- Reserved and detached from others
- Calm, collected and analytical
- Extremely logical and rational
- Original and independent
- Natural leaders, but will follow those they can fully support
- Creative, ingenious, innovative, and resourceful
- Work best alone, and prefer to work alone

More so than any other personality type, INTJs are brilliant when it comes to grasping complex theories and applying them to problems to come up with long-term strategies. Since this type of "strategizing" is the central focus and drive of the INTJ, there is a happy match between desire and ability in this type. Accordingly, the INTJ is happiest and most effective in careers which allow this type of processing, and which promote an environment in which the INTJ is given a lot of autonomy over their daily lives.

The following list of professions is built on our impressions of careers which would be especially suitable for an INTJ. It is meant to be a starting place, rather than an exhaustive list. There are no guarantees that any or all of the careers listed here would be appropriate for you, or that your best career match is among those listed.

Possible Career Paths for the INTJ:

Academic Curriculum Designer
Administrator
Aeronautical Engineer
Aerospace Engineer
Animator
Anthropologist
Architect
Artist
Archivist
Astronomer
Attorney
Auditor
Biologist
Biomedical Researcher/Engineer
Broadcast Engineer
Budget Analyst
Business Analyst
Cardiologist
Cardiovascular Technician
Chemical Engineer
City Manager
Civil Engineer
College Professor
Columnist, Critic, Or Commentator
Computer Engineer
Computer Programmer
Computer Security Specialist
Computer Systems Analyst
Coroner
Corrections Officer
Credit Analyst
Criminologist Or Ballistics Expert
Curator
Database Administrator
Dentist

Design Engineer
Designer
Desktop Publishing Specialist
Economist
Editor/Art Director
Education Consultant
Electrical/Electronic Technician
Engineer
Environmental Planner/Scientist
Exhibit Designer/Builder
Financial Analyst
Financial Planner
Geneticist
Graphic Designer
Human Resources Manager
Information Services Developer
Intellectual Properties Attorney
Intelligence Specialist
International Banker
Inventor
Investment Banker
Java Programmer/Analyst
Judge
Life Scientist
Local Area Network (LAN) Administrator
Management Consultant
Manager
Mathematician
Metallurgical Engineer
Microbiologist
Mortgage Broker
Musician
Network Administrator
Network Integration Specialist
Neurologist

News Analyst/Writer
Nuclear Engineer
Operations Research Analyst
Pathologist
Pharmaceutical Researcher
Pharmacologist
Photographer
Physical Scientist
Physicist
Pilot
Private Sector Executive
Psychiatrist
Psychologist
Real Estate Appraiser

Social Scientist
Software And Systems
Researcher/Developer
Strategic Planner
Surgeon
Systems Administrator
Systems Analyst
Teacher
Telecommunications Security Provider
Treasurer Or Controller
Web Developer
Webmaster
Writer/Editor

More information can be found on the Internet by searching for "careers for INTJ**" **

INTJ Relationships

INTJs believe in constant growth in relationships and strive for independence for themselves and their mates. They are constantly embarking on "fix-up" projects to improve the overall quality of their lives and relationships. They take their commitments seriously, but are open to redefining their vows, if they see something which may prove to be an improvement over the existing understanding. INTJs are not likely to be "touchy-feely" and overly affirming with their mates or children and may at times be somewhat insensitive to their emotional needs. However, INTJs are in general extremely capable and intelligent individuals who strive to always be their best and be moving in a positive direction. If they apply these basic goals to their personal relationships, they likely to enjoy happy and healthy interaction with their families and friends.

INTJ Strengths

- Not threatened by conflict or criticism
- Usually, self-confident
- Take their relationships and commitments seriously
- Generally, extremely intelligent, and capable
- Able to leave a relationship which should be ended, although they may dwell on it in their minds for a while afterwards
- Interested in "optimizing" their relationships
- Good listeners

INTJ Weaknesses

- Not naturally in tune with the feelings of others; may be insensitive at times
- May tend to respond to conflict with logic and reason, rather than the desired emotional support
- Not naturally good at expressing feelings and affections
- Tendency to believe that they're always right

56

- Tendency to be unwilling or unable to accept blame
- Their constant quest to improve everything may be taxing on relationships
- Tend to hold back part of themselves

Potential Problem Areas

With any gift of strength, there is an associated weakness. Without "bad", there would be no "good." Without "difficult", there would be no "easy." We value our strengths, but we often curse and ignore our weaknesses. To grow as a person and get what we want out of life, we must not only capitalize upon our strengths, but also face our weaknesses and deal with them. That means taking a hard look at our personality type's potential problem areas.

INTJs are rare and intelligent people with many special gifts. This should be kept in mind as you read some of the more negative material about INTJ weaknesses. Remember that these weaknesses are natural. We offer this information to enact positive change, rather than as blatant criticism. We want you to grow into your full potential and be the happiest and most successful person that you can become.

Most of the weaker characteristics that are found in INTJs are due to their dominant function (Introverted iNtuition) overtaking their personality to the point that the other forces in their personality exist merely to serve the purposes of Introverted iNtuition. In such cases, an INTJ may show some or all of the following weaknesses in varying degrees:

- May be unaware (and sometimes uncaring) of how they come across to others
- May quickly dismiss input from others without really considering it
- May apply their judgment more often towards others, rather than towards themselves
- With their ability to see an issue from many sides, they may always find others at fault for problems in their own lives
- May look at external ideas and people with the primary purpose of finding fault
- May take pride in their ability to be critical and find fault in people and things
- May have unrealistic and/or unreasonable expectations of others
- May be intolerant of weaknesses in others
- May believe that they're always right
- May be cuttingly derisive and sarcastic towards others
- May have an intense and quick temper
- May hold grudges, and have difficulty forgiving people
- May be wishy-washy and unsure how to act in situations that require quick decision making
- May have difficulty communicating their thoughts and feelings to others
- May see so many tangents everywhere that they can't stay focused on the bottom line or the big picture

Ten Rules to Live By to Achieve INTJ Success

1. *Feed Your Strengths!* Do things that allow your brilliant intuition and logical abilities to flourish. Explore the fascinating worlds of science, mathematics, law, and medicine. Give your mind an outlet for its exceptional analytical abilities and watch them grow.

2. *Face Your Weaknesses!* See your weaknesses for what they are and seek to overcome them. Especially, strive to use your judgment against your internal ideas and intuitions, rather than as a means of disregarding other people's ideas.

3. *Talk Through Your Thoughts.* You need to step through your intuitions in order to put them into perspective. Give yourself time to do this and take advantage of discussing ideas with others. You'll find externalizing your internal intuitions to be a valuable exercise. If you don't have someone to discuss your ideas with, try expressing your ideas clearly in writing.

4. *Take In Everything.* Don't dismiss ideas prematurely because you don't respect the person generating the ideas, or because you think you already know it all. After all, everybody has something to offer, and nobody knows everything. Steven Covey says it so well when he says: "Seek first to understand, and then to be understood."

5. *When You Get Angry, You Lose.* Your passion and intensity are strong assets but can be very harmful if you allow yourself to fall into the "Anger Trap." Remember that Anger is destructive to your personal relationships. Work through your anger before you impress it upon others, or you will likely find yourself alone. Disagreements and disappointments can only be handled effectively in a non-personal and dispassionate manner.

6. *Respect Your Need For Intellectual Compatibility.* Don't expect yourself to be a "touchy-feely" or "warm-fuzzy" person. Realize that your most ardent bonds with others will start with the head, rather than the heart. Be aware of other's emotional needs and express your genuine love and respect for them in terms that are real to YOU. Be yourself.

7. *Be Accountable For Yourself.* Don't blame the problems in your life on other people. Look inwardly for solutions. No one has more control over your life than you have.

8. *Be Humble.* Judge yourself at least as harshly as you judge others.

9. *Assume the Best.* Don't distress yourself and others by dwelling on the dark side of everything. Just as there is a positive charge for every negative charge, there is a light side to every dark side. Remember that positive situations are created by positive attitudes. Expect the best, and the best will come forward.

10. *Don't Get Isolated!* Recognize the value that the external world represents to you and interact with it in the style that's natural to you. Join clubs and internet e-mail lists that house in-depth discussions of topics that you're interested in. Seek and foster friendships with others of like competence and capacity for understanding. Extravert in your own style.

Careers for ENTP Personality Types

Enthusiastic, outgoing, analytic idea people. ENTPs often are multitalented characters interested in nearly everything. Independent, non-conforming and sometimes a little rebellious and confrontational, this type may be an inspiration to others who will follow the ENTP guru into uncharted waters--sometimes shark-infested! Many ENTPs have a hard time dealing with long-range planning, facing practical constraints to their projects, coping with structured working situations and authority figures, and keeping their interpersonal relationships on an even keel. Entrepreneurship may meet this type's needs when more conventional business situations are unattractive. The ENTP has the ability to succeed in a variety of careers--and may move from one to another over the course of a lifetime--always seeking new opportunities and retreating from projects which have degenerated to hum-drum routine. Whatever their chosen field of endeavor, from sales to science, art or writing to psychology, ENTPs always play the role of visionary, promoter, marketer, and instigator.

Whether you're a young adult trying to find your place in the world, or a not-so-young adult trying to find out if you're moving along the right path, it's important to understand yourself and the personality traits which will impact your likeliness to succeed or fail at various careers. It's equally important to understand what is really important to you. When armed with an understanding of your strengths and weaknesses, and an awareness of what you truly value, you are in an excellent position to pick a career which you will find rewarding.

ENTPs generally have the following traits:

- Project-oriented
- Enjoy generating ideas and theories
- Creative and ingenious
- Bright and capable
- Flexible and Diverse
- Excellent communication skills
- Enjoy debating issues with other people
- Excellent people skills
- Natural leaders, but do not like to control people
- Resist being controlled by people
- Lively and energetic; able to motivate others
- Highly value knowledge and competence
- Logical, rational thinkers
- Able to grasp difficult concepts and theories
- Enjoy solving difficult problems
- Dislike confining schedules and environments
- Dislike routine, detailed tasks

ENTPs are fortunate in that they have a wide range of capabilities. They are generally good at anything which has captured their interest. ENTPs are likely to be successful in many different careers. Since they have a lot of options open to them, ENTPs will do well to choose professions which allow them a lot of personal freedom where they can use their creativity to generate new ideas and solve problems. They will not be completely happy in positions which are regimented or confining.

The following list of professions is built on our impressions of careers which would be especially suitable for an ENTP. It is meant to be a starting place, rather than an exhaustive list. There are no guarantees that any or all of the careers listed here would be appropriate for you, or that your best career match is among those listed.

Possible Career Paths for the ENTP:

Actor	Internet Marketer
Advertising Creative Director	Inventor
Aeronautical Engineer	Investment Banker/Broker
Art Director (Magazine)	Journalist
Athletic Coach Or Scout	Lawyer
Attorney (Litigator)	Literary Agent
Broadcast News Analyst	Logistics Consultant—Manufacturing
Business Manager	Management Consultant
Chiropractor	Marketing Researcher/Planner
Columnist, Critic, Or Commentator	Motivational Speaker
Computer Analyst	Network Integration Specialist
Computer Programmer	(Telecommunications)
Computer Specialist	New Business Developer—Information
Computer Systems Analyst	Services
Copy Writer	Ombudsperson
Corrections Officer	Optometrist
Creative Director—Multimedia Team	Outplacement Consultant
Creative Writer	Personnel Systems Developer
Credit Investigator	Photographer
Criminalist Or Ballistics Expert	Political Analyst
Desktop Publisher/Specialist	Political Manager
Detective	Politician
Director—Stage Or Motion Pictures	Producer
Diversity Manager/Trainer	Property Manager—
Educational Psychologist	Commercial/Residential
Employee Relations Specialist	Psychologist
Engineer	Public Relations Specialist
Entrepreneur	Radio/TV Talk Show Host
Environmental Scientist	Real Estate Agent/Developer
Event Planner	Reporter Or Correspondent
Financial Planner	Restaurant/Bar Owner
Foreign Language Teacher	Sales Agent—Securities/Commodities
Home Economist	Security Analyst
Hotel/Motel Manager	Social Scientist
Human Resources Recruiter	Speech Pathologist
Industrial Design Manager	Sports Marketer
Informational-Graphics Designer	Strategic Planner
International Marketing	Student Personnel Administrator
Internet Architect	Technical Trainer

University Or College President   Venture Capitalist
Urban/Regional Planner

**More information can be found on the Internet by searching for "careers for INTJ" **

ENTP Relationships

Typically good-natured, upbeat, and laid-back, ENTPs can be delightful people to be around. They get a lot of enjoyment and satisfaction from interacting with others, and especially enjoy discussing and debating theories and concepts which interest them. They may be prone to initiate arguments because they so enjoy the debate. They are generally fun-loving and gregarious and can be quite charming. They have a problem with sometimes neglecting their close relationships when they become involved in the pursuit of a new idea or plan.

ENTP Strengths

- Enthusiastic, upbeat, and popular
- Can be very charming
- Excellent communication skills
- Extremely interested in self-improvement and growth in their relationships
- Laid-back and flexible, usually easy to get along with
- Big idea people, always working on a grand scheme or idea
- Usually good at making money, although not so good at managing it
- Take their commitments and relationships very seriously
- Able to move on with their lives after leaving a relationship

ENTP Weaknesses

- Always excited by anything new, they may change partners frequently
- Tendency to not follow through on their plans and ideas
- Their love of debate may cause them to provoke arguments
- Big risk-takers and big spenders, not usually good at managing money
- Although they take their commitments seriously, they tend to abandon their relationships which no longer offer opportunity for growth

Potential Problem Areas

With any gift of strength, there is an associated weakness. Without "bad", there would be no "good." Without "difficult", there would be no "easy." We value our strengths, but we often curse and ignore our weaknesses. To grow as a person and get what we want out of life, we must not only capitalize upon our strengths, but also face our weaknesses and deal with them. That means taking a hard look at our personality type's potential problem areas.

Most of the weaker characteristics that are found in ENTPs are due to their dominant function of Extraverted Intuition overtaking the personality to the point that the other functions exist merely to serve its purposes. In such cases, an ENTP may show some or all of the following weaknesses in varying degrees:

- The inability to maintain a comfortable situation or relationship once its possibilities have been realized or exhausted.
- A tendency to consider careful or meticulous thinkers as unworthy plodders or time wasters.
- Blindness to the needs and feelings of others not directly involved in the ENTP's current area of interest.
- A lack of sensitivity to the feelings and ways of those who might need reassurance, security, or commitment.
- The inability to deal carefully and calmly with the finer details of a situation or work in progress.
- Becoming overly annoyed by minor setbacks or small things that have to be set right before the goal can be realized.
- A tendency to be arrogant or boastful, or to demean those who cannot see the same answers.
- Can often find themselves in bad situations by too quickly taking a big step forward or by being "too smart for their own good."

Ten Rules to Live By to Achieve ENTP Success

1. *Feed Your Strengths!* Realize your gift of seeing past the obvious brings you a great capacity to reward yourself and others through your cleverness. Make sure you engage in activities, and which can expose this potential at its most valuable level.
2. *Face Your Weaknesses!* We all have weaknesses. Recognizing your weaknesses for what they are (without beating yourself up) will give you the power to change your life for the better.
3. *Talk Through Your Perceptions.* Discussing what you see with others will them understand where you are coming from and offer you the chance to discover the ways in which their input can balance your ideas.
4. *Relax And Enjoy The View.* Take the time to consider what you have; the gifts life has already brought to you. Try and discover the value and importance of those constant day-to-day things which support and nourish you.
5. *Be Aware Of Others.* Understand that everyone has their own lives and their own perspectives. Everyone has something to offer. Try to identify people's personality type.

6. ***Recognize Norms And Structures Are Necessary.*** Remember that without the support and constancy of others, no one can follow their dreams. The path you walk was laid by others, each of its steppingstones created to fulfill a different part of the human need for constancy and security. Without this support structure, you cannot go far.

7. ***Get Out Of Your Comfort Zone.*** Understand that the only way to grow is to get outside of your comfort zone. If you're feeling uncomfortable in situation because it seems to be going nowhere, that's good! That's an opportunity for growth.

8. ***Identify And Express Your Feelings.*** You may have a hard time understanding your feelings. It's important that you try to figure this out. Don't let people down. If you determine that you value a person, tell them so every time you think of it. This is the best way to make them feel secure in your affections, and so to promote a long-lasting relationship.

9. ***Be Accountable For Yourself.*** Remember that no one has more control over your life than you have. Don't be a victim.

10. ***Assume The Best But Be Wary.*** Your positive attitude nearly always creates positive situations. Just remember: to make them lasting and worthwhile you must build them on solid, carefully planned foundations.

Careers for INTP Personality Types

Private, intellectual, impersonal, analytical, and reflective, the INTP appears to value ideas, principles, and abstract thinking above all else. This logical type seeks to understand and explain the universe--not to control it! Higher education often holds a particular appeal to this type who tends to acquire degrees and amass knowledge over the entire course of life. Abstract or theoretical subjects are usually the INTP's cup of tea, and academic or research careers may seem attractive to this type. From science and math to economics and philosophy: just name the discipline, and you'll find INTPs perched on the loftiest rungs of theory and analysis. In whatever field they choose, INTPs take on the role of visionary, scientist, or architect, and they usually prefer to make their contributions in relative solitude. The mundane details of life may be the INTP's undoing since this type lives in a world guided by intuitive thinking. Often perceived to be arrogant and aloof, the quiet and sometimes reclusive INTP may have to struggle in the personal realm, as well, for feelings are not this type's natural forte.

Whether you're a young adult trying to find your place in the world, or a not-so-young adult trying to find out if you're moving along the right path, it's important to understand yourself and the personality traits which will impact your likeliness to succeed or fail at various careers. It's equally important to understand what is really important to you. When armed with an understanding of your strengths and weaknesses, and an awareness of what you truly value, you are in an excellent position to pick a career which you will find rewarding.

INTPs generally have the following traits:

- Love theory and abstract ideas
- Truth Seekers - they want to understand things by analyzing underlying principles and structures
- Value knowledge and competence above all else
- Have very high standards for performance, which they apply to themselves
- Independent and original, possibly eccentric
- Work best alone, and value autonomy
- Have no desire to lead or follow
- Dislike mundane detail
- Not particularly interested in the practical application of their work
- Creative and insightful
- Future-oriented
- Usually brilliant and ingenious
- Trust their own insights and opinions above others
- Live primarily inside their own minds, and may appear to be detached and uninvolved with other people

INTPs have a special gift with generating and analyzing theories and possibilities to prove or disprove them. They have a great deal of insight and are creative thinkers, which allows them to quickly grasp complex abstract thoughts. They also have exceptional logical and rational reasoning skills, which allows them to thoroughly analyze theories to discover the Truth about them. Since the INTP is driven to seek clarity in the world, we have a happy match of desire and ability in this personality type. INTPs will be happiest in careers which allow them a great deal of autonomy in which they can work primarily alone on developing and analyzing complex theories and abstractions, with the goal of their work being the discovery of a truth, rather than the discovery of a practical application.

The following list of professions is built on our impressions of careers which would be especially suitable for an INTP. It is meant to be a starting place, rather than an exhaustive list. There are no guarantees that any or all of the careers listed here would be appropriate for you, or that your best career match is among those listed.

Possible Career Paths for the INTP:

Anthropologist	Computer Engineer
Archaeologist	Computer Programmer
Architect	Computer Security Specialist
Artist	Computer Software Designer
Astronomer	Constitutional Lawyer
Biomedical Engineer/Researcher	Consultant
Biophysicist	Corporate Finance Attorney
Business Analyst	Creative Writer
College Administrator	Desktop Publishing Specialist
College Professor (Graduate Programs)	Economist
Columnist, Critic, Commentator	Entertainer/Dancer
Computer Animator	Entertainment Agent

Entrepreneur
Financial Analyst/Planner
Forensic Researcher
Forestry And Park Ranger
Geneticist
Historian
Information Services Developer
Informational-Graphics Designer
Intellectual Property Attorney
Intelligence Specialist
Internet Architect
Interpreter/Translator
Inventor
Investigator
Investment Banker
Java Programmer/Analyst
Judge
Lawyer
Legal Mediator
Logician
Mathematician
Microbiologist
Music Arranger/Orchestrator
Musician
Network Administrator

Network Integration Specialist
Neurologist
Occupational Therapist
Pharmaceutical Researcher
Pharmacist
Philosopher
Photographer
Physicist
Plastic Surgeon
Psychiatrist
Psychologist/Psychoanalyst
Research And Development Specialist
Respiratory Therapist
Scientist (Chemistry/Biology)
Social Scientist
Software Designer
Software Developer
Strategic Planner
Systems Analyst/Database Manager
Technical Writer
Venture Capitalist
Veterinarian
Web Developer
Webmaster

**More information can be found on the Internet by searching for "careers for INTP" **

INTP Relationships

INTPs live rich worlds inside their minds, which are full of imagination and excitement. Consequently, they sometimes find the external world pales in comparison. This may result in a lack of motivation to form and maintain relationships. INTPs are not likely to have a very large circle of significant relationships in their lives. They're much more likely to have a few very close relationships, which they hold in great esteem and with great affection. Since the INTP's primary focus and attention is turned inwards, aimed towards seeking clarity from abstract ideas, they are not naturally tuned into others' emotional feelings and needs. They tend to be difficult to get to know well and hold back parts of themselves until the other person has proven themselves "worthy" of hearing the INTP's thoughts. Holding Knowledge and Brain Power above all else in importance, the INTP will choose to be around people who they consider to be intelligent. Once the INTP has committed themselves to a relationship, they tend to be very faithful and loyal, and form affectionate attachments which are pure and straight-forward. The INTP has no interest or understanding of game-playing with regards to relationships. However, if something happens which the INTP considers irreconcilable, they will leave the relationship and not look back.

INTP Strengths

- They feel love and affection for those close to them which is almost childlike in its purity
- Generally laid-back and easy-going, willing to defer to their mates
- Approach things which interest them very enthusiastically
- Richly imaginative and creative
- Do not feel personally threatened by conflict or criticism
- Usually are not demanding, with simple daily needs

INTP Weaknesses

- Not naturally in tune with others' feelings, slow to respond to emotional needs
- Not naturally good at expressing their own feelings and emotions
- Tend to be suspicious and distrusting of others
- Not usually good at practical matters, such as money management, unless their work involves these concerns
- They have difficulty leaving bad relationships
- Tend to "blow off" conflict situations by ignoring them, or else they "blow up" in heated anger

Potential Problem Areas

With any gift of strength, there is an associated weakness. Without "bad", there would be no "good." Without "difficult", there would be no "easy." We value our strengths, but we often curse and ignore our weaknesses. To grow as a person and get what we want out of life, we must not only capitalize upon our strengths, but also face our weaknesses and deal with them. That means taking a hard look at our personality type's potential problem areas.

Most of the weaker characteristics that are found in INTPs are due to their dominant function of Introverted Thinking overtaking the personality to the point that all of the other functions exist merely to serve the purposes of Introverted Thinking. In such cases, an INTP may show some or all of the following weaknesses in varying degrees:

- The INTP gets "stuck in a rut" and only does those things that are known and comfortable to the INTP.
- The INTP resists and rejects anything that doesn't support their own experiential understanding of the world. If they perceive that something is not logical, they reject it as unimportant.
- They reject people who think or live differently than themselves.
- They may be extremely caustic and insulting to others.
- They may become isolated from society.
- They may become overly paranoid about social organizations and institutions trying to control them.
- They may unknowingly or uncaringly hurt people's feelings.

- They may be completely unaware of how to express their inner world to others in a meaningful way.
- They may be completely unaware of the type of communication that is often desirable and (to some degree) expected in an intimate relationship. If they are aware of the kinds of things that are appropriate to say and do to foster emotional bonding, they may be unable to appreciate the value of such actions. They may feel too vulnerable to express themselves in this fashion, and so reject the entire idea.
- If pushed beyond their comfort level to form commitments or emotional bonds, they may reject a relationship entirely.
- Under stress, they may show intense emotions that seem disproportionate to the situation.
- They may not recognize basic social principles, such as appropriate dress and general behavior

Ten Rules to Live By to Achieve INTP Success

1. *Feed Your Strengths!* Realize your gift at mastering logical problems and situations and give yourself plenty of opportunities to exercise your abilities. Much of your sense of well-being will come from these experiences.
2. *Face Your Weaknesses!* We all have weaknesses. Recognizing your weaknesses for what they are (without beating yourself up) will give you the power to change your life for the better.
3. *Talk About Your Thoughts.* Discussing your ideas and perceptions with others will help you to develop your Extraverted INtuition, and thus your understanding of the world. How well you use your auxiliary function is very important to your overall health and happiness.
4. *Listen To Everything.* Try not to dismiss anything immediately. Let it soak in, and then apply judgment. Try not to dismiss things that are a logical - they are not illogical.
5. *Be Aware Of Others.* Understand that everyone has their own lives and their own perspectives. Everyone has something to offer. Try to identify people's personality type.
6. *Recognize Social Principles.* Realize that our society functions around some basic social principles, and that our society would fail unless those principles are recognized and upheld. In a democracy, people vote. At a red stoplight, people stop. If people stopped voting because it wasn't important them, who would be in power? If people stopped stopping at red stop lights because it didn't fit into their plans, how could we drive safely? Your priorities and plans are important, but you must recognize that the external world's agenda is also important. Don't dismiss the importance of principles that don't affect your life directly.
7. *Get Out Of Your Comfort Zone.* Understand that the only way to grow is to get outside of your comfort zone. If you're uncomfortable with an idea or situation because you're not sure how to act, that's good! That's an opportunity for growth.
8. *Identify And Express Your Feelings.* You may have a hard time understanding how you feel about someone. It's important that you do figure this out. Don't lead someone on with your ambivalence. If you determine that you value the person, tell them so

every time you think of it. This is the best way to make them feel secure in your affections, and so to promote a long-lasting relationship.

9. ***Be Accountable For Yourself.*** Remember that no one has more control over your life than you have. Don't be a victim.

10. ***Assume The Best.*** Don't distress yourself with fear and dark expectations. Remember that a positive attitude often creates positive situations.

Careers for ENFJ Personality Types

As an ENFJ, you're primary mode of living is focused externally, where you deal with things according to how you feel about them, or how they fit into your personal value system. Your secondary mode is internal, where you take things in primarily via your intuition.

ENFJs are people-focused individuals. They live in the world of people possibilities. More so than any other type, they have excellent people skills. They understand and care about people and have a special talent for bringing out the best in others. ENFJ's main interest in life is giving love, support, and a good time to other people. They are focused on understanding, supporting, and encouraging others. They make things happen for people and get their best personal satisfaction from this.

Whether you're a young adult trying to find your place in the world, or a not-so-young adult trying to find out if you're moving along the right path, it's important to understand yourself and the personality traits which will impact your likeliness to succeed or fail at various careers. It's equally important to understand what is really important to you. When armed with an understanding of your strengths and weaknesses, and an awareness of what you truly value, you are in an excellent position to pick a career which you will find rewarding.

ENFJs generally have the following traits:

- Genuinely and warmly interested in people
- Value people's feelings
- Value structure and organization
- Value harmony, and good at creating it
- Exceptionally good people skills
- Dislike impersonal logic and analysis
- Strong organizational capabilities
- Loyal and honest
- Creative and imaginative
- Enjoy variety and new challenges
- Get personal satisfaction from helping others
- Extremely sensitive to criticism and discord
- Need approval from others to feel good about themselves
- The flexibility of these characteristics leaves the ENFJ a lot of leeway in choosing a profession. As long as they're in a supportive environment in which they can work with people and are presented with sufficient diverse challenges to stimulate their creativity, they should do very well.

68

The following list of professions is built on our impressions of careers which would be especially suitable for an ENFJ. It is meant to be a starting place, rather than an exhaustive list. There are no guarantees that any or all of the careers listed here would be appropriate for you, or that your best career match is among those listed here.

Possible Career Paths for the ENFJ:

Adult Day Care Coordinator
Advertising Account Executive
Bilingual Education Teacher
Career Counselor
Child Life Specialist
Child Welfare Worker
Chiropractor
Clergy/Minister
Coach
College Or University Administrator
College Professor (Humanities)
Communications Director
Composer
Content Editor For Web Site
Copy Writer
Corporate Outplacement Counselor
Corporate/Team Trainer
Counselor
Customer Relations Manager
Dental Hygienist
Desktop Publishing Specialist
Dietitian/Nutritionist
Diplomat
Director Of Assisted Care Facility
Director Of Childcare Facility
Editor
Educational Program Director
Educational Psychologist
Entertainer/Artist
Event Planner
Executive (Small Business)
Fund-Raiser
Graphic Artist
Guidance Counselor
Holistic Health Practitioner
Hotel And Restaurant Manager
Human Resource Development Trainer
Human Resources Recruiter
Interpreter/Translator

Labor Relations Manager
Librarian
Management Consultant
Marketing Executive (Broadcast Industry)
Marketing Manager
Multimedia Producer
Music Director
Newscaster
Nonprofit Organization Director
Occupational Therapist
Optometrist
Outplacement Consultant
Parent Instructor, Child Development
Personnel Recruiter
Philanthropic Consultant
Planned-Giving Officer
Politician
Probation Officer
Project Manager
Psychologist
Public Health Educator
Public Relations Specialist
Recreational Director
Reporter And Correspondent
Sales Manager/Trainer
Set Designer
Social And Community Service Director
Social Scientist
Social Worker
Sociologist
Special Education Teacher
Speech-Language Pathologist/Audiologist
Staff Advocate (Technology Consultant)
Teacher (Health, Art, Drama, English)
Therapist
Travel Agent
TV Producer
Urban And Regional Planner
Writer/Journalist

**More information can be found on the Internet by searching for "careers for ENFJ" **

ENFJ Relationships

ENFJs put a lot of effort and enthusiasm into their relationships. To some extent, the ENFJ defines themselves by the closeness and authenticity of their personal relationships and are therefore highly invested in the business of relationships. They have very good people skills and are affectionate and considerate. They are warmly affirming and nurturing. The excel at bringing out the best in others, and warmly supporting them. They want responding affirmation from their relationships, although they have a problem asking for it. When a situation calls for it, the ENFJ will become very sharp and critical. After having made their point, they will return to their natural, warm selves. They may have a tendency to "smother" their loved ones but are generally highly valued for their genuine warmth and caring natures.

ENFJ Strengths

Most ENFJs will exhibit the following strengths with regards to relationship issues:

- Good verbal communication skills
- Very perceptive about people's thoughts and motives
- Motivational, inspirational; bring out the best in others
- Warmly affectionate and affirming
- Fun to be with - lively sense of humor, dramatic, energetic, optimistic
- Good money skills
- Able to "move on" after a love relationship has failed (although they blame themselves)
- Loyal and committed - they want lifelong relationships
- Strive for "win-win" situations
- Driven to meet other's needs

ENFJ Weaknesses

Most ENFJs will exhibit the following weaknesses with regards to relationships issues:

- Tendency to be smothering and over-protective
- Tendency to be controlling and/or manipulative
- Don't pay enough attention to their own needs
- Tend to be critical of opinions and attitudes which don't match their own
- Sometimes unaware of social appropriateness or protocol
- Extremely sensitive to conflict, with a tendency to sweep things under the rug as an avoidance tactic
- Tendency to blame themselves when things go wrong, and not give themselves credit when things go right
- Their sharply defined value systems make them unwavering in some areas
- They may be so attuned to what is socially accepted or expected that they're unable to assess whether something is "right" or "wrong" outside of what their social circle expects.

Potential Problem Areas

With any gift of strength, there is an associated weakness. Without "bad", there would be no "good." Without "difficult", there would be no "easy." We value our strengths, but we often curse and ignore our weaknesses. To grow as a person and get what we want out of life, we must not only capitalize upon our strengths, but also face our weaknesses and deal with them. That means taking a hard look at our personality type's potential problem areas.

Most of the weaker characteristics found in ENFJs are due to their dominant Extraverted Feeling overvaluing what they see as objective values in the external world and thereby judging too much by the needs of others, or by appearances. This is primarily due to the ENFJ having not fully adapted their Introverted Intuitive function sufficiently for them to be able to discern the vast range of ways in which they might be being missing the underlying needs within themselves and being misled by such appearances. The ENFJ naturally looks outward to find value and satisfaction, and whilst it is essential that this direction be taken to fulfill their primary needs of relation and comfort, without the supportive balance of a well-developed Intuitive function, ENFJs can overvalue the external world to the point where they lose sight of themselves, becoming fixed in their judgments about people and the world. In such cases, the ENFJ will tend to live in a rigid - and to others, somewhat surreal - world of definite values which often seems "overstated" or obsessively connected to other people or human situations.

Ten Rules to Live By to Achieve ENFJ Success

1. *Feed Your Strengths!* Make sure you have opportunities to involve yourself with others in situations where your input is valued.
2. *Face Your Weaknesses!* Realize and accept that some traits are strengths, and some are weaknesses. By facing your weaknesses, you can overcome them, and they will have less power over you.
3. *Express Your Feelings.* Understand that your feelings are as important as others are in the overall situation. Without your feelings and needs being valued the best result is not realized, so value and speak to your own feelings as much as you value those of others.
4. *Make Decisions.* Don't be afraid to have an opinion. You need to know show others the qualities and potentials you can see are worthy of action.
5. *Smile at Criticism.* Try to see why disagreement and discord indicate the differences between people and use this as an opportunity to make your value judgments useful for growth, because that's exactly what they are. Try not to feel responsible for another's criticism but try to hear it and understand the feelings and images it engenders within you. Then you may see a path not only to agreement but to a shared and truly valuable end.
6. *Be Aware of Others.* Remember that there are 15 other personality types out there who see things differently than you see them. Most of your problems with other people are easier to deal with if you try to understand the other person's perspective.
7. *Be Aware of Yourself.* Don't stint your own needs for the sake of others too much. Realize you are an important focus. If you do not fulfill your own needs, how will continue to be effective and how will others know you are true to your beliefs?
8. *Be Gentle in Your Expectations.* It is easy for you to see the value in others but stressing this too much can drive them away. Try to show that you understand their

71

fears and limitations and lead them gently to see how you feel: lead them gently into understanding and love.

9. *Assume the Best.* Don't distress yourself by feeling that your values are lost upon others – they are not. Perhaps it just has to sit with them too. Let the situation resolve itself and never stop believing that love is the true answer.

10. *When in Doubt, Ask Questions!* Don't assume that the lack of feedback is the same thing as negative feedback. If you need feedback and don't have any, ask for it.

Careers for INFJ Personality Types

INFJs are intuitive, caring, quiet and peace-loving: deep and complex people who may seem equally at home dealing with the personal and analytical spheres of life. The interior world of vision and ideas is this type's most comfortable domain, but some degree of human connection is essential for the INFJ's happiness, a potential conflict for this type. Articulate, empathetic, and idealistic, INFJs often say they just know things, they know them directly, and they may not be able to tell you how or why! INFJs seem to be able to feel others' feelings vicariously and sense the good and evil in situations: an almost psychic ability which may be an asset in many "people professions." Spiritual, sensitive, and committed, INFJs enjoy being of service to others. Once this type's goals are set and the mind is made up, no argument based solely on reason and practicality is likely to divert the passionate INFJ from a mission or chosen project. Whether this characteristic manifests itself as admirable tenacity or bull-headed stubbornness may determine the individual INFJ's potential for life success.

Whether you're a young adult trying to find your place in the world, or a not-so-young adult trying to find out if you're moving along the right path, it's important to understand yourself and the personality traits which will impact your likeliness to succeed or fail at various careers. It's equally important to understand what is really important to you. When armed with an understanding of your strengths and weaknesses, and an awareness of what you truly value, you are in an excellent position to pick a career which you will find rewarding.

INFJs generally have the following traits:

- Intuitively understand people and situations
- Idealistic
- Highly principled
- Complex and deep
- Natural leaders
- Sensitive and compassionate towards people
- Service-oriented
- Future-oriented
- Value deep, authentic relationships
- Reserved about expressing their true selves
- Dislike dealing with details unless they enhance or promote their vision
- Constantly seeking meaning and purpose in everything
- Creative and visionary
- Intense and tightly-wound
- Can work logically and rationally - use their intuition to understand the goal and work backwards towards it

The INFJ is a special individual who needs more out of a career than a job. They need to feel as if everything they do in their lives is in sync with their strong value systems - with what they believe to be right. Accordingly, the INFJ should choose a career in which they're able to live their daily lives in accordance with their deeply held principles, and which supports them in their life quest to be doing something meaningful. Since INFJs have such strong value systems, and persistent intuitive visions which lend them a sense of "knowing", they do best in positions in which they are leaders, rather than followers. Although they can happily follow individuals who are leading in a direction which the INFJ fully supports, they will very unhappily be following in any other situation.

The following list of professions is built on our impressions of careers which would be especially suitable for an INFJ. It is meant to be a starting place, rather than an exhaustive list. There are no guarantees that any or all of the careers listed here would be appropriate for you, or that your best career match is among those listed.

Possible Career Paths for the INFJ:

Adult Day Care Coordinator
Architect
Artist
Bilingual Education Teacher
Career Counselor
Child Life Specialist
Child Welfare Counselor
Chiropractor
Clergy
Coach
Corporate/Team Trainer
Corrective Therapist
Costume And Wardrobe Specialist
Crisis Hotline Operator
Customer Relations Manager
Desktop Publisher/Editor
Dietitian/Nutritionist
Director Of Religious Education
Director, Social Service Agency
Diversity Manager, Human Resources
Documentary Filmmaker
Editor/Art Director (Web Sites)
Editor/Art Director (Magazines)
Educational Consultant
Educational Program Director
Educational Software Developer
Employee Assistance Program
Coordinator
Environmental Lawyer
Exhibit Designer
Film Editor
Freelance Media Planner
Fund-Raising Director
Genealogist
Grant Coordinator
Health Care Administrator
Holistic Health Practitioner
Home Economist
Human Resource Manager/Recruiter
Informational-Graphics Designer

Interior Designer
Interpreter/Translator
Job Analyst
Legal Mediator
Legislative Assistant
Librarian/Informational Specialist
Marketer
Massage Therapist
Mediator/Conflict Resolver
Medical Doctor
Mental Health Counselor
Merchandise Designer/Displayer
Multimedia Producer
Museum Research Worker
Musician
Novelist
Occupational Therapist
Organizational Development Consultant
Parenting Instructor, Child Development
Course
Pharmacist
Philanthropic Consultant
Photographer
Planned-Giving Officer
Playwright
Poet
Preferred Customer Sales Representative
Psychiatrist
Psychologist
Public Health Educator
Religious Worker
Set Designer
Social Scientist
Social Worker
Special Education Teacher
Speech-Language Pathologist/Audiologist
Staff Advocate (Technology Consultant)
Substance Abuse Counselor
Teacher (Liberal Arts)
Universal Design Architect

**More information can be found on the Internet by searching for "careers for INFJ" **

INFJ Relationships

INFJs are warm and affirming people who are usually also deep and complex. They're likely to seek out and promote relationships that are intense and meaningful. They tend to be perfectionists and are always striving for the Ultimate Relationship. For the most part, this is a positive feature, but sometimes works against the INFJ if they fall into the habit of moving from relationship to relationship, always in search of a more perfect partner. In general, the INFJ is a deeply warm and caring person who is highly invested in the health of their close relationships and puts forth a lot of effort to make them positive. They are valued by those close to them for these special qualities. They seek long-term, lifelong relationships, although they don't always find them.

INFJ Strengths

- Warm and affirming by nature
- Dedicated to achieving the ultimate relationship
- Sensitive and concerned for others' feelings
- Usually have good communication skills, especially written
- Take their commitments very seriously, and seek lifelong relationships
- Have very high expectations for themselves and others (both a strength and weakness)
- Good listeners
- Are able to move on after a relationship has ended (once they're sure it's over)

INFJ Weaknesses

- Tendency to hold back part of themselves
- Not good with money or practical day-to-day life necessities
- Extreme dislike of conflict and criticism
- Have very high expectations for themselves and others (both a strength and weakness)
- Have difficulty leaving a bad relationship

Potential Problem Areas

With any gift of strength, there is an associated weakness. Without "bad", there would be no "good." Without "difficult", there would be no "easy." We value our strengths, but we often curse and ignore our weaknesses. To grow as a person and get what we want out of life, we must not only capitalize upon our strengths, but also face our weaknesses and deal with them. That means taking a hard look at our personality type's potential problem areas.

INFJs are rare and intelligent people with many special gifts. This should be kept in mind as you read some of the more negative material about INFJ weaknesses. Remember that these weaknesses are natural. We offer this information to enact positive change, rather than as blatant criticism. We want you to grow into your full potential and be the happiest and most successful person that you can become.

Most of the weaker characteristics that are found in INFJs are due to their dominant function (Introverted iNtuition) overtaking their personality to the point that the other forces in their personality exist merely to serve the purposes of Introverted iNtuition. In such cases, an INFJ may show some or all of the following weaknesses in varying degrees:

- May be unaware (and sometimes uncaring) of how they come across to others
- May quickly dismiss input from others without really considering it
- May apply their judgment more often towards others, rather than towards themselves
- With their ability to see an issue from many sides, they may always find others at fault for any problems in their lives
- May have unrealistic and/or unreasonable expectations of others
- May be intolerant of weaknesses in others
- May believe that they're always right
- May be obsessive and passionate about details that may be unimportant to the big picture
- May be cuttingly derisive and sarcastic towards others
- May have an intense and quick temper
- May be tense, wound up, have high blood pressure, and find it difficult to relax
- May hold grudges, and have difficulty forgiving people
- May be wishy-washy and unsure how to act in situations that require quick decision making
- May have difficulty communicating their thoughts and feelings to others
- May see so many tangents everywhere that they can't stay focused on the bottom line or the big picture

Ten Rules to Live By to Achieve INFJ Success

1. *Feed Your Strengths!* Do things that allow your brilliant intuition and service-oriented manner to flourish.
2. *Face Your Weaknesses!* See your weaknesses for what they are and seek to overcome them. Especially, strive to use your judgment against your internal ideas and intuitions, rather than as a means of disregarding other people's ideas.
3. *Talk Through Your Thoughts.* You need to step through your intuitions in order to put them into perspective. Give yourself time to do this and take advantage of discussing ideas with others. You'll find externalizing your internal intuitions to be a valuable exercise.
4. *Take in Everything.* Don't dismiss ideas prematurely because you don't respect the person generating the ideas, or because you think you already know it all. After all, everybody has something to offer, and nobody knows everything. Steven Covey says it so well when he says: "Seek first to understand, and then to be understood."
5. *Your passion and intensity are strong assets but can be very harmful if you allow yourself to fall into the "Anger Trap."* Remember that Anger is destructive to your personal relationships. Work through your anger before you impress it upon others, or you will likely find yourself alone. Disagreements and disappointments can only be handled effectively in a non-personal and dispassionate manner.
6. *Keep Your Eye on the Big Picture.* Watch out for your tendency to become obsessed with details. If you find yourself feeling very, very strongly about a small detail, take a big step back and make sure that you can still see the goal. You're not going to get there if you get mired in the details.
7. *Be Accountable for Yourself.* Don't blame the problems in your life on other people. Look inwardly for solutions. No one has more control over your life than you have.
8. *Be Humble.* Judge yourself at least as harshly as you judge others.
9. *Assume the Best.* Don't distress yourself and others by dwelling on the dark side of everything. Just as there is a positive charge for every negative charge, there is a light side to every dark side. Remember that positive situations are created by positive attitudes. Expect the best, and the best will come forward.
10. *Relax!* Do yourself a favor and learn how to effectively unwind. Get exercise and restful sleep. Take vacations. Engage in relaxing activities. Take care of yourself and your loved ones by learning to let go of your passion and intensity for a respite.

Careers for ENFP Personality Types

ENFPs are open-minded, imaginative, caring, and outgoing. They thrive on the drama of life by observing everything enthusiastically and associating meaning and human motive with all they survey. To the ENFP, no life event is devoid of significance--a belief which may justify others' perception of them as hyper alert, oversensitive and even suspicious at times. Charming, interactive, charismatic, communicative, and ingenious, ENFPs often are expansive in their approach to life, love and work--multitalented individuals who may succeed in a number of creative endeavors, so long as a strong human element is present. "Do this, do that!" jobs demanding strict compliance with rules, regulations and procedures, and attention to logic, facts and details are stressful for most ENFPs. Their characteristically short attention span and diversity of interests may sabotage their accomplishment in enterprises demanding tenacity and single-mindedness. This type's natural gift for inspiring others often is their salvation: the projects ENFPs start may be completed by their followers.

Whether you're a young adult trying to find your place in the world, or a not-so-young adult trying to find out if you're moving along the right path, it's important to understand yourself and the personality traits which will impact your likeliness to succeed or fail at various careers. It's equally important to understand what is really important to you. When armed with an understanding of your strengths and weaknesses, and an awareness of what you truly value, you are in an excellent position to pick a career which you will find rewarding.

ENFPs generally have the following traits:

- Project-oriented
- Bright and capable
- Warmly, genuinely interested in people, great people skills
- Extremely intuitive and perceptive about people
- Able to relate to people on their own level
- Service-oriented; likely to put the needs of others above their own
- Future-oriented
- Dislike performing routine tasks
- Need approval and appreciation from others
- Cooperative and friendly
- Creative and energetic
- Well-developed verbal and written communication skills
- Natural leaders, but do not like to control people
- Resist being controlled by others
- Can work logically and rationally - use their intuition to understand the goal and work backwards towards it
- Usually able to grasp difficult concepts and theories

ENFPs are lucky in that they're good a quite a lot of different things. An ENFP can generally achieve a good degree of success at anything which has interested them. However, ENFPs get bored rather easily and are not naturally good at following things through to completion. Accordingly, they should avoid jobs which require performing a lot of detailed, routine-oriented tasks. They will do best in professions which allow them to creatively generate new

78

ideas and deal closely with people. They will not be happy in positions which are confining and regimented.

The following list of professions is built on our impressions of careers which would be especially suitable for an ENFP. It is meant to be a starting place, rather than an exhaustive list. There are no guarantees that any or all of the careers listed here would be appropriate for you, or that your best career match is among those listed.

Possible Career Paths for the ENFP:

Advertising Account Manager/Executive
Advertising Creative Director
Anthropologist
Artist
Bilingual Education Teacher
Broadcast News Analyst
Career Counselor
Cartoonist Or Animator
Character Actor
Chemist
Child Life Specialist
Child Welfare Counselor
Chiropractor
Coach
Columnist
Computer Programmer/Specialist
Computer Systems Analyst
Consultant
Corporate/Team Trainer
Corrections Officer
Costume And Wardrobe Designer
Counseling Psychologist
Customer Relations Manager
Desktop Publisher
Dietitian/Nutritionist
Documentary Filmmaker
Early Childhood Education Teacher
Editor/Art Director (Web Sites)
Education Software Developer
Educational Psychologist
Employee Assistance Program Counselor
Entrepreneur
Environmental Attorney
Event Planner
Exhibit Designer
High School Guidance Counselor
Holistic Health Practitioner
Human Resources Manager/Trainer
Information-Graphics Designer

Insurance Agent
Interior Designer
Inventor
Labor Relations Manager
Legal Mediator
Librarian
Marketing Consultant
Marketing Executive (Radio, TV, Cable)
Medical Assistant
Merchandise Planner
Multimedia Producer
Musician/Composer
Newscaster
Occupational Therapist
Ombudsperson
Parent Instructor, Child Development
Personnel Recruiter
Philanthropic Consultant
Physical Therapist
Planned-Giving Officer
Politician
Public Health Educator
Public Relations Specialist
Publicist
Rehabilitation Worker
Religious Worker/Pastoral Counselor
Reporter/Editor/Art Director (Magazine)
Research Assistant
Residential Housing Director
Restauranteur
Screenwriter/Playwright
Sales (Intangibles/Ideas)
Social Psychologist
Social Scientist
Social Worker
Special Education Teacher
Speech-Language Pathologist/Audiologist
Staff Advocate (Technology Consultant)
Strategic Planner

Teacher (Humanities)	Travel Agent
Television Producer	Urban Regional Planner
Theater Director	

**More information can be found on the Internet by searching for "careers for ENFP" **

ENFP Relationships

ENFPs take their relationships very seriously, but also approach them with a childlike enthusiasm and energy. They seek and demand authenticity and depth in their personal relationships and will put forth a lot of effort into making things work out. They are warm, considerate, affirming, nurturing, and highly invested in the health of the relationship. They have excellent interpersonal skills and are able to inspire and motivate others to be the best that they can be. Energetic and effervescent, the ENFP is sometimes smothering in their enthusiasm, but are generally highly valued for their genuine warmth and high ideals.

ENFP Strengths

Most ENFPs will exhibit the following strengths with regards to relationships issues:

- Good communication skills
- Very perceptive about people's thought and motives
- Motivational, inspirational; bring out the best in others
- Warmly affectionate and affirming
- Fun to be with - lively sense of humor, dramatic, energetic, optimistic
- Strive for "win-win" situations
- Driven to meet other's needs
- Usually loyal and dedicated

ENFP Weaknesses

Most ENFPs will exhibit the following weaknesses with regards to relationship issues:

- Tendency to be smothering
- Their enthusiasm may lead them to be unrealistic
- Uninterested in dealing with "mundane" matters such as cleaning, paying bills, etc.
- Hold onto bad relationships long after they've turned bad
- Extreme dislike of conflict
- Extreme dislike of criticism
- Don't pay attention to their own needs
- Constant quest for the perfect relationship may make them change relationships frequently
- May become bored easily
- Have difficulty scolding or punishing others

Potential Problem Areas

With any gift of strength, there is an associated weakness. Without "bad", there would be no "good." Without "difficult", there would be no "easy." We value our strengths, but we often curse and ignore our weaknesses. To grow as a person and get what we want out of life, we must not only capitalize upon our strengths, but also face our weaknesses and deal with them. That means taking a hard look at our personality type's potential problem areas.

Most of the weaker characteristics found in ENFPs are due to their dominant Extraverted Intuition overshadowing the personality to the extent that they don't apply judgment to anything. Or they may use their primary judging function (Introverted Feeling) to support the agenda of Extraverted Intuition, i.e., to rationalize and support the idea of welcoming all experiences and accepting all individuals. In such cases, an ENFP may show some or all of the following weaknesses in varying degree:

- May be what many would call a "sucker," vulnerable to schemers and con artists.
- May get themselves into dangerous situations because they're too eager to push the envelope of their understanding, and not willing to apply judgment to anything.
- May feel intense anger towards people who criticize them or try to control them. But will be unable to express the anger. Left unexpressed, the anger may fester and simmer and become destructive.
- May blame their problems on other people, using logic and ration to defend themselves against the world.
- May develop strong negative judgments that are difficult to unseed against people who they perceive have been oppressive to them.
- May get involved with drugs, alcohol, or promiscuity, and generally seek mindless experiences and sensations.
- May skip from relationship to relationship without the ability to commit.
- May start projects but be unable to finish them.
- May be unable to stick to a career or job for any length of time.

Ten Rules to Live By to Achieve ENFP Success

1. *Feed Your Strengths!* Make sure you have opportunities to have new experiences to feel your quest of understanding the world.

2. *Face Your Weaknesses!* Realize and accept that some traits are strengths, and some are weaknesses. By facing your weaknesses, you can overcome them, and they will have less power over you.

3. *Express Your Feelings.* Don't let anger get bottled up inside you. If you have strong feelings, sort them out and express them, or they may become destructive!

4. *Make Decisions.* Don't be afraid to have an opinion. You need to know how you feel about things in order to be effective.

5. *Smile at Criticism.* Try to see disagreement and discord as an opportunity for growth, because that's exactly what it is. Try not to become overly defensive towards criticism; try to hear it and judge it objectively.

6. *Be Aware of Others.* Remember that there are 15 other personality types out there who see things differently than you see them. Most of your problems with other people are easier to deal with if you try to understand the other person's perspective.

7. *Be Aware of Yourself.* Don't stint your own needs for the sake of others too much. Realize you are an important focus. If you do not fulfill your own needs, how will continue to be effective and how will others know you are true to your beliefs?

8. *Be Accountable for Yourself.* Don't waste mental energy finding blame in other's behavior, or in identifying yourself as a victim. You have more control over your life than any other person has.

9. *Assume the Best.* Don't distress yourself by assuming the worst. Remember that a positive attitude creates positive situations.

10. *When in Doubt, Ask Questions!* Don't assume that the lack of feedback is the same thing as negative feedback. If you need feedback and don't have any, ask for it.

Careers for INFP Personality Types

INFPs are quiet, creative, sensitive, and perceptive souls who often strike others as shy, reserved, and cool. These folks have a rare capacity for deep caring and commitment--both to the people and causes they idealize. INFPs guide their behavior by a strong inner sense of values, rather than by conventional logic and reason. Forced to cope with this facts-and-figures "real" world we inhabit, INFPs may appear to have been imported from another galaxy! They gravitate toward creative or human service careers which allow them to use their instinctive sense of empathy and remarkable communication skills. Strongly religious, spiritual, or philosophical people, INFPs may see the purpose of their lives as an inner journey, quest, or personal unfolding. More practical or rational types may tend to discredit the INFP's sources of understanding as mystical. The search for a soul mate is a preoccupation for many INFPs, who must balance their need for privacy and peace with their yearning for human connection. If there seems to be an air of sadness in the INFP's spirit, blame it on this type's longing for the perfect in all things.

Whether you're a young adult trying to find your place in the world, or a not-so-young adult trying to find out if you're moving along the right path, it's important to understand yourself and the personality traits which will impact your likeliness to succeed or fail at various careers. It's equally important to understand what is really important to you. When armed with an understanding of your strengths and weaknesses, and an awareness of what you truly value, you are in an excellent position to pick a career which you will find rewarding.

INFPs generally have the following traits:

- Strong value systems
- Warmly interested in people
- Service-oriented, usually putting the needs of others above their own
- Loyal and devoted to people and causes
- Future-oriented
- Growth-oriented; always want to be growing in a positive direction
- Creative and inspirational
- Flexible and laid-back, unless a ruling principle is violated
- Sensitive and complex
- Dislike dealing with details and routine work
- Original and individualistic - "out of the mainstream"
- Excellent written communication skills
- Prefer to work alone, and may have problems working on teams
- Value deep and authentic relationships
- Want to be seen and appreciated for who they are
- The INFP is a special, sensitive individual who needs a career which is more than a job.

The INFP needs to feel that everything they do in their lives is in accordance with their strongly felt value systems and is moving them and/or others in a positive, growth-oriented direction. They are driven to do something meaningful and purposeful with their lives. The INFP will be happiest in careers which allow them to live their daily lives in accordance with

83

their values, and which work towards the greater good of humanity. It's worth mentioning that nearly all of the truly great writers in the world have been INFPs.

The following list of professions is built on our impressions of careers which would be especially suitable for an INFP. It is meant to be a starting place, rather than an exhaustive list. There are no guarantees that any or all of the careers listed here would be appropriate for you, or that your best career match is among those listed.

Possible Career Paths for the INFP:

Actor
Architect
Artist
Bilingual Education Teacher
Biological Scientist
Career Counselor
Child Life Specialist
Child Welfare Counselor
Clinical Psychologist
Coach
College Professor (Humanities, Arts)
Composer
Consultant—Team Building/Conflict
Resolution
Corporate Team Trainer
Counselor
Curator
Customer Relations Manager
Desktop Publisher
Dietitian/Nutritionist
Diversity Manager—Human Resources
Early Childhood Education Teacher
Editor
Educational Consultant
Educational Software Developer
Employee Assistance Counselor
Engagement Manager
Entertainer
Ethicist
Fashion Designer
Film Editor
Genealogist
Geneticist
Grant Coordinator
Health Technician

Holistic Health Practitioner
Home Health Social Worker
Human Resources Development Specialist
Human Resources Recruiter
Industrial Organization Psychologist
Informational Graphic Designer
Interior Designer
Journalist
Labor Relations Specialist
Legal Mediator
Librarian
Manual Arts Therapist
Minister/Priest
Missionary
Multimedia Producer
Musician
Occupational Therapist
Outplacement Consultant
Philanthropic Consultant
Physical Therapist
Planned-Giving Officer
Psychologist
Public Health Educator
Public Health Nurse
Religious Educator
Religious Worker
Researcher
Set Designer
Social Scientist
Social Worker
Special Education Teacher
Speech-Language Pathologist/Audiologist
Staff Advocate (Technology Consultant)
Translator/Interpreter
Writer (Poet, Novelist)

**More information can be found on the Internet by searching for "careers for INFP" **

INFP Relationships

INFPs present a calm, pleasant face to the world. They appear to be tranquil and peaceful to others, with simple desires. In fact, the INFP internally feels his or her life intensely. In the relationship arena, this causes them to have a very deep capacity for love and caring which is not frequently found with such intensity in the other types. The INFP does not devote their intense feelings towards just anyone and are relatively reserved about expressing their inner-most feelings. They reserve their deepest love and caring for a select few who are closest to them. INFPs are generally laid-back, supportive and nurturing in their close relationships. With Introverted Feeling dominating their personality, they're very sensitive and in tune with people's feelings and feel genuine concern and caring for others. Slow to trust others and cautious in the beginning of a relationship, an INFP will be fiercely loyal once they are committed. With their strong inner core of values, they are intense individuals who value depth and authenticity in their relationships and hold those who understand and accept the INFP's perspectives in especially high regard. INFPs are usually adaptable and congenial, unless one of their ruling principles has been violated, in which case they stop adapting and become staunch defenders of their values. They will be uncharacteristically harsh and rigid in such a situation.

INFP Strengths

Most INFPs will exhibit the following strengths with regards to relationship issues:

- Warmly concerned and caring towards others
- Sensitive and perceptive about what others are feeling
- Loyal and committed - they want lifelong relationships
- Deep capacity for love and caring
- Driven to meet other's needs
- Strive for "win-win" situations
- Nurturing, supportive and encouraging
- Likely to recognize and appreciate other's need for space
- Able to express themselves well
- Flexible and diverse

INFP Weaknesses

Most INFPs will exhibit the following weaknesses with regards to relationship issues:

- May tend to be shy and reserved
- Don't like to have their "space" invaded
- Extreme dislike of conflict
- Extreme dislike of criticism
- Strong need to receive praise and positive affirmation
- May react very emotionally to stressful situations
- Have difficulty leaving a bad relationship
- Have difficulty scolding or punishing others
- Tend to be reserved about expressing their feelings
- Perfectionist tendencies may cause them to not give themselves enough credit
- Tendency to blame themselves for problems, and hold everything on their own shoulders

Potential Problem Areas

With any gift of strength, there is an associated weakness. Without "bad", there would be no "good." Without "difficult", there would be no "easy." We value our strengths, but we often curse and ignore our weaknesses. To grow as a person and get what we want out of life, we must not only capitalize upon our strengths, but also face our weaknesses and deal with them. That means taking a hard look at our personality type's potential problem areas.

INFPs are rare, intelligent, creative beings with many special gifts. I would like for the INFP to keep in mind some of the many positive things associated with being an INFP as they read some of this more negative material. Also remember that the weaknesses associated with being an INFP are natural to your type. Although it may be depressing to read about your type's weaknesses, please remember that we offer this information to enact positive change. We want people to grow into their own potential, and to live happy and successful lives.

Most of the weaker characteristics that are found in INFPs are due to their dominant Feeling function overshadowing the rest of their personality. When the dominant function of Introverted Feeling overshadows everything else, the INFP can't use Extraverted iNtuition to take in information in a truly objective fashion. In such cases, an INFP may show some or all of the following weaknesses in varying degrees:

- May be extremely sensitive to any kind of criticism
- May perceive criticism where none was intended
- May have skewed or unrealistic ideas about reality
- May be unable to acknowledge or hear anything that goes against their personal ideas and opinions
- May blame their problems on other people, seeing themselves as victims who are treated unfairly
- May have great anger, and show this anger with rash outpourings of bad temper
- May be unaware of appropriate social behavior
- May be oblivious to their personal appearance, or to appropriate dress
- May come across as eccentric, or perhaps even generally strange to others, without being aware of it
- May be unable to see or understand anyone else's point of view
- May value their own opinions and feelings far above others
- May be unaware of how their behavior affects others
- May be oblivious to other people's need
- May feel overwhelmed with tension and stress when someone expresses disagreement with the INFP, or disapproval of the INFP
- May develop strong judgments that are difficult to unseed against people who they perceive have been oppressive or suppressive to them
- Under great stress, may obsess about details that are unimportant to the big picture of things
- Under stress, may obsessively brood over a problem repeatedly
- May have unreasonable expectations of others
- May have difficulty maintaining close relationships, due to unreasonable expectations

Ten Rules to Live By to Achieve INFP Success

1. *Feed Your Strengths!* Encourage your natural artistic abilities and creativity. Nourish your spirituality. Give yourself opportunities to help the needy or underprivileged.
2. *Face Your Weaknesses!* Realize and accept that some traits are strengths, and some are weaknesses. Facing and dealing with your weaknesses doesn't mean that you have to change who you are, it means that you want to be the best You possible. By facing your weaknesses, you are honoring your true self, rather than attacking yourself.
3. *Express Your Feelings.* Don't let unexpressed emotions build up inside of you. If you have strong feelings, sort them out and express them, Don't let them build up inside you to the point where they become unmanageable!
4. *Listen to Everything.* Try not to dismiss anything immediately. Let everything soak in for a while, then apply judgment.
5. *Smile at Criticism.* Remember that people will not always agree with you or understand you, even if they value you greatly. Try to see disagreement and criticism as an opportunity for growth. In fact, that is exactly what it is.
6. *Be Aware of Others.* Remember that there are 15 other personality types out there who see things differently than you see them. Try to identify other people's types. Try to understand their perspectives.
7. *Be Accountable for Yourself.* Remember that YOU have more control over your life than any other person has.
8. *Be Gentle in Your Expectations.* You will always be disappointed with others if you expect too much of them. Being disappointed with another person is the best way to drive them away. Treat others with the same gentleness that you would like to be treated with.
9. *Assume the Best.* Don't distress yourself by assuming the worst. Remember that a positive attitude often creates positive situations.
10. *When in Doubt, Ask Questions!* Don't assume that the lack of feedback is the same thing as negative feedback. If you need feedback and don't have any, ask for it.

Financial Reality Check

So, will a career that you enjoy or are interested in bear the cost of the lifestyle you want outside of work? Here is a simple way to find out. Evaluate the samples below and then build your own budget and find out your minimum salary you are looking for.

Single Adult Sample

Category	Monthly Costs
Food	$260
Housing	$800
Health Care	$92
Transportation	$490
Other Necessities	$207
Net Taxes	$286
Total Monthly Costs	$2,135
Total Annual Costs	$25,620
Hourly Wage Needed	$12.32

*Hourly wage for 1 fulltime employee

Married Adult Sample

Category	Monthly Costs
Food	$445
Housing	$850
Health Care	$277
Transportation	$739
Other Necessities	$289
Net Taxes	$412
Total Monthly Costs	$2,945
Total Annual Costs	$35,340
Hourly Wage Needed	$8.49

*Hourly wage for 2 fulltime employees

Category	Monthly Costs
Food	_____
Housing	_____
Health Care	_____
Transportation	_____
Net Taxes	_____
_____	_____
_____	_____
_____	_____
_____	_____
_____	_____
_____	_____
_____	_____
_____	_____

Total Monthly Costs _____

Total Annual Costs _____
(Multiply Monthly cost by 12)

Hourly Wage Needed _____
(Divide Annual Costs by 2080)

> List all of your expenses such as food, rent or mortgage, health care, transportation, taxes, entertainment, and debt payments.
>
> Some of these expenses are the same amount each month, while others vary.
>
> For those expenses, try to budget a set amount for each month.
>
> Review past bills and receipts to determine the amount that you spend each month.

Application

Sample Application for Employment

Here is a sample application that you can fill out to have the information ready when you do apply. Use this to copy and paste where the formatting, spelling and grammar has been reviewed to ease the application.

Title of Specific Position for Which You Are Applying		Date of Application	Date Available for Work	
Last Name	First Name	Middle Initial		
Mailing Address	City	State		Zip
Email Address	Are you 18 years of age or over?	Primary Phone		
County of Residence	Yes No If No, Date of Birth	Second Phone		

Education

Did you graduate from high school or receive a GED?

___ No   ___ Yes   School Attended:

Name and Location of College, University, Technical Schools	Did you Graduate?	Certificate or Degree	Course of Study
	Yes No		
	Yes No		
	Yes No		

Employment
(List employment history, but do not provide dates of employment for jobs held more than five years ago.)

Employing Firm		From	Month	Year	To	Month	Year
Address		Reason for Leaving					
Phone Number	Supervisor						
Your Title	Supervisor's Title	May we contact this employer? Yes No If No, explain.					

Principal Responsibilities

Employing Firm		From	Month	Year	To	Month	Year
Address		Reason for Leaving					
Phone Number	Supervisor						
Your Title	Supervisor's Title	May we contact this employer? _ Yes _ No If No, explain.					

Principal Responsibilities

Employing Firm		From	Month	Year	To	Month	Year
Address		Reason for Leaving					
Phone Number	Supervisor						
Your Title	Supervisor's Title	May we contact this employer?					
		___ Yes ___ No ___ If No, explain.					

Principal Responsibilities

Are you willing to work overtime? ☐Yes ☐No	What shift would you prefer? (If applicable) 1st 2nd 3rd	Are you willing to work other shifts? ☐No ☐Yes If Yes, what shifts? 1st 2nd 3rd

Job Relevant Volunteer and Unpaid Work Experience

Kind of Volunteer Activity (Do not specify organization.)	Major Responsibilities	# Hours/Week	Length of Service

Describe any additional experience or training that qualifies you for this job

References

(Give us the names of three people outside of relatives who can be contacted regarding your qualifications, work habits and character.)

Name	Present Address	Phone	Position and relation to your work

Military

Did you serve in the military service of this country and separate under honorable conditions from any branch of the armed forces of the U.S. after having served on active duty for 181 consecutive days or by reason of disability incurred while serving on active duty?   __Yes __No

Additional information

Cover Letter

A cover letter is a requirement for some job applications and a great idea for others. Now use this opportunity as a chance to tell the employer why you are perfect for this job. Tell them about how you are a match, how you're interested, or how your experience can be related. When writing cover letters, your paragraphs should be concise and focused on your qualifications for the job.

A cover letter should include three paragraphs:
- Introduction
- Body/Selling Pitch
- Conclusion

The first paragraph explains why you are writing. It is the first impression and a basic explanation of whom you are and why you are writing. It is also acceptable to describe how you found the position or why you are interested in the job. If you can research and find out whom the hiring manager is then address the letter to them directly and address their needs that you meet. Here is where you name drop someone that is recommending that you apply. If you are trying to have an employee or someone in their circle speak on your behalf, say something like, "after discussing your position with Mr. Ronald Jones I was excited to apply and find out more about this opportunity."

The second paragraph, known as the body of the cover letter. This can be multiple paragraphs explaining why you are qualified for the position. This is the part of the letter where it is most appropriate to highlight your experience, skills, and attributes that make you a perfect candidate for the position. Don't copy information from your resume; rather focus on the most important factors that make you desirable that are hard to fit in your resume like your personality, passions, goals or interests in the position. Think of this as where your soft skills can find their way into your application.

The third paragraph is a brief conclusion thanking the employer for their time and consideration. Be sure to reiterate your interest in the position and describe how you will next follow up.

Be sure to leave a space between each paragraph.

Dear Hiring Manager,

I would like to express my interest in a position as the editorial assistant for your publishing company.

As a recent graduate with writing, editing, and administrative experience, I believe I am a strong candidate for a position at the 123 Publishing Company.

You specify that you are looking for someone with strong writing skills. As an English major, a writing tutor, and an editorial intern for both a government magazine and a college marketing office, I have become a skilled writer with a variety of experience.

My maturity, practical experience, and eagerness to enter the publishing business will make me an excellent editorial assistant. I would love to begin my career with your company, and I am confident that I would be a beneficial addition to the 123 Publishing Company.

I have enclosed my resume and will call within the next week to see if we might arrange a time to speak together.

Thank you so much for your time and consideration.

Resume

Identify key things employers look for
- Relevant and basic skills and experience needed to do the job
- Accomplishments/Results
- Something that shows them how well you use your skills
- Personality traits, work habits
- Show them who you are and what makes you effective

Formats
- Chronological
  - Highlights recent employment ~ de-emphasizing previous jobs
  - Good for consistent employment history
- Functional
  - Highlight skills, experience and accomplishments
  - Organized by functions or skills
  - Good for first-time job seekers or gaps in employment
- Combination
  - Best of both formats ~ highlights skills and accomplishments
  - List work history in chronological order

Basic Rules
- Keep it brief
- Have a visual impact
- Check your grammar and spelling
- Ensure integrity
- Target your resume
- Focus on the skills they are looking for
- Use their key words and phrases
- Print on quality paper

References can be included on the resume or on a separate attachment if required
- References can come from a wide variety of people, including current or former:
  - Supervisors or managers
  - Colleagues
  - Customers or clients
  - Mentors
  - Teachers or academic advisors
  - Community/religious leaders
  - Volunteer coordinators

Resume Tips

- Generally, list only the last 10-15 years of experience or the last 3-5 jobs in most cases.
- Include an "Additional Relevant Experience" section without dates for experience more than 15 years old.
- List employer name, city and state only; do not include street addresses.
- Dates of employment: you may list the years only; months are not needed. Keep on the right-hand side.
- Include job title of each position and put it in bold.
- List duties <u>and</u> accomplishments in short, bulleted phrases (easy to read) or in short paragraphs. Focus on accomplishments to make your resume more powerful. Use numbers for results whenever possible.
- Use as many skill words as possible yet be concise.
- Use strong action verbs to begin sentences or phrases (i.e., developed, designed, etc. Present tense verbs for current job, past tense verbs for past jobs.)
- Avoid the use of personal pronouns, "I" or "My" and articles such as "a, an," and "the."
- Try to avoid using "duties included" or "responsibilities included."
- Include military experience to fill gaps in employment or to support the target job.
- "Civilianize" military language to transferable skills to match employer's needs. (Example: change "War College" to "advanced training.")

Analyzing Past Work Tasks for Results & Accomplishments

- *Every work task you completed on your job had some type of result or impact on something else.*
- *Listing the results of what you did is the best way to strengthen your resume and interviewing stories.*
- *Always talk about what you did in terms of results:*

Examples of how numbers and percentages can make a statement measureable. It paints a picture that can be seeing regardless of if someone understands your experiences.

1. Thoughtfully assisted customers in making product selections, which increased overall satisfaction.
2. Designed marketing and promotional brochures which improved brand awareness and increased market share by 10%.
3. Thoroughly trained 18 new clerical staff, resulting in standardized application of procedures and improved customer satisfaction.
4. Researched and chose new office supplies vendor, which resulted in decreased costs and higher quality of supplies. Saved approximately 25% or $3000 in first year.
5. Established and maintained a good rapport with various internal departments, which impacted productivity and overall staff effectiveness.
6. Created a new procedure for escalating customer complaints, resulting in increased customer satisfaction and significant repeat business.

Resume Accomplishment Examples

Customer Service
- Accomplished Customer Service professional with 5 years experience in the financial industry.
- Skilled in Microsoft Word, Excel and Teams. Familiar with PowerPoint for remote customer engagement connection.
- Consistently acknowledged by management for excellent skills in efficiently managing workflow, communicating clearly and professionally, and being able to quickly learn new information.

Assistant Teacher
- Four years' experience in tutoring K-6 students.
- Skilled in using a variety of teaching strategies and techniques to foster student motivation and implement methods that accommodate differences in developmental levels and learning styles among diverse students.
- Recognized for having a trustworthy, safe, creative, calming nature to handle any classroom situation.
- Dependable, organized, efficient, patient, loving nature with a sense of humor.
- Proven skills in MS Word, and knowledge in Excel and PowerPoint. CPR and First Aid Certified.

Administrative Assistant
- Detail-oriented administrative assistant with two years experienced in large corporate settings.
- Skilled in MS Word and Excel, familiar with PowerPoint. Above average 10 key skills.
- Quick learner; always motivated to learn new skills.
- Regularly sought out for problem solving assistance by coworkers and supervisors in every job.
- Bilingual, Vietnamese

Maintenance and Repair
- 10 years experience providing maintenance and upkeep for assisted living sites.
- Take initiative to figure things out on my own and to follow up on quality of repairs.
- Known for responding patiently and quickly to resident service requests.
- Takes pride in getting frequent compliments from staff, residents, and families of residents for cheerful and caring attitude.

Assembly/Production Worker
- Over 10 years' experience in operating a wide variety of machines.
- 8 years' forklift driving experience.
- Quick learner, good at working with my hands and with many types of machines.
- Known for being a hard worker who meets daily production rates without sacrificing quality or safety.

(Mixed background with a lot of different job titles)
- Dependable, hard worker, who always gets there on time and finishes work quickly.
- Friendly and confident individual who enjoys learning new things.
- Flexible team player with good problem-solving skills, motivated in completing tasks thoroughly.
- Fluent in Somali, English and Kiswahili.

Search your previous and prospective careers on the information websites we used for your interests to create your accomplishment lists.

Education

- List in order of relevance, not necessarily by date.
- List high school diploma or GED only if you do not have any college education.
- College degrees: list name of institution, city, state, degree earned and field of study.
- Leave degree completion dates off to eliminate possible age discrimination. However, if degree is recent, listing the date may increase its value.
- You don't have to include advanced degrees if unrelated to target job. (Always include Bachelor's degrees.)
- You may want to include current enrollment in school or training and list projected completion date.
- For post-secondary education that did not result in a degree, list the school, city and state along with the type of coursework completed.
- Always list some type of education or training you've completed.
- Include employer-sponsored training, workshops and seminars if related to target job.
- If recent graduate with no related work experience, list education before work experience.

Examples: Name High School, City ST
High School Diploma

Area Learning Center, City ST
General Education Diploma

Hometown Community College, City, ST
Coursework in Business Administration (1 year)

Hometown Community College, City, ST
Welding Certificate Program
(Currently enrolled; completion expected by May 20XX)

University of State, City, ST
B.A. in Business Management, Economics minor

<u>**Seminars and On-the-Job Training**</u>
Communication Skills in the Workplace
Supervisory Skills
Conflict Resolution Skills

Hobbies/Personal Interests
- Include only if employment-related and not controversial (such as political or religious).
- Sometimes you may want to list them if intriguing or shows something about who you are.

Volunteer or Other Experience
- Include only experience that relates to the target job and is not controversial (such as political or religious).
- Use same format as used in the Work Experience section, listing title, agency, city and state.

Organizations/Memberships
- List professional organization memberships if they are related to your target job.
- Avoid listing controversial organizations, such as religious or political, unless related to target job.

JOHN SMITH   (123) 456-7890

123 South Village Road, City, ST 12345   name@email.com

Objective   The Objective is a brief statement that expresses a goal for employment or college.

Highlight Skills Any skills you possess that are in the job posting or you would like to highlight

Employment

Cashier Stop & Shop   Years or Duration

Copy the relatable bullets from http://www.onetonline.org/

Go to http://www.onetonline.org/

Type in the job title you are researching for professional descriptions

Copy and paste the relatable comments - Edit as necessary

Sample:

- Received payment by cash, check, credit cards, vouchers, or automatic debits.
- Assisted customers by providing information and resolving their complaints.
- Established or identified prices of goods, services or admission, and tabulated bills using calculators, cash registers, or optical price scanners.
- Greeted customers entering establishment.
- Answered customers' questions and provided information on procedures or policies.
- Maintained clean and orderly checkout areas and completed other general cleaning duties, such as mopping floors and emptying trash cans.
- Stocked shelves and marked prices on shelves and items.

Education   Anywhere High School   City, ST

Honors/Awards

High School Honor Roll   Grade 10 – 12
National Honor Society   Grade 10 – 11

Extracurricular

Student Council   Grades 10 – 12
Varsity Basketball   Grades 9 – 12
HS Connect Leader   Grade 11
Freshman Band   Grade 9

Other   Use this category for specific activities or interests that may not fall under another heading. Examples are: Computer or other Special Skills, Languages, Travel, etc. Change the heading to reflect the content of your category.

Community Service/Volunteer Experience

Big Brother / Big Sister   Grades 9 – 11
Relay for Life participant   Grades 9 – 10

Interests

Guitar, photography, skiing, biking, reading

Interview

Total interview preparation system…. TIPS

Prepare For An Interview

- Get and prepare appropriate interviewing clothes.
- Learn and practice confidence and attitude tricks.
- Prepare a strong "tell me about yourself" speech, related to the job applied for.
- Prepare a story for every line on your resume and every skill asked for in the job description.
- Prepare for difficult questions (the ones you hope they won't ask!)
- Prepare to offer descriptions of your skills if the interviewer is doing all of the talking.
- Find out the name(s) and titles of interviewer(s), panel or individually?
- Arrive early.
- Chat with the first contact person.
- Remember to make eye contact and to smile when meeting everyone!
- Ask them to describe the ideal candidate, and then give a story describing how you fit the description.
- Send a Thank You note or letter to everyone who interviewed you.

Know The Employer—Understand The Job

- Major product(s) or services(s)
- Size (number of employees)
- Location(s)
- Who are their clients? What do the clients think of them?
- Who are their competitors?
- Who are their suppliers?
- What does the organizational structure look like? Who are the key people in their organization? What are their roles?
- What are their problems?
- What is their financial standing? (or their source of funding if they are a non-profit)
- What key qualifications/skills/attributes/traits is the employer seeking?

Know Yourself

- Which of your qualifications will be most important to the employer?
- What are your greatest strengths?
- What things about your background make you stand out?
- Which of your career/job highlights should be emphasized?
- What characteristics do you possess that make you a strong candidate?
- What are your strongest areas of skill and expertise? Knowledge? Experience?
- What are your three greatest career accomplishments?
- Can you quantify these accomplishments in numerical or other specific terms?

Know Your Remote Interview Challenges

- Is any of your background visibly distracting?
- Test the software before the interview, practice with a person you trust and will give feedback.
- Ensure your network will support the bandwidth needed.
- Have a backup plan if you lose connection.
- Inform everyone in the area that you are interviewing, for support and an uninterrupted time.

Prepare & Practice Your Answers to Common Questions

Question	Hint	Your answer
Big picture		
Tell me about yourself	Use your elevator speech.	
Tell me about your last job	Focus on how it relates.	
Tell me about your career so far	Seeking patterns and themes.	
Please describe a typical day	Looking for what really happens.	
Tell me about your ideal job	Looking for key motivation.	
Strengths		
What has made you successful?	Examples and reasons for success.	
What interests you most about this job?	Show your motivation.	
What is your greatest strength?	What you think you're good at.	
Tell me about when you were particularly challenged	Challenge brings out the real person.	
What have you done that you are proud of?	Motivation and concern for self.	
Why should I employ you?	Show fit and motivation.	
Possible weaknesses		
What are your weaknesses?	Admit non-important weaknesses.	
What did you like least about that job?	Checking the range of your motivation.	
Have you ever lost your job?	Show positive attitude.	
Stress		
Can you work under pressure?	Demonstrate self-control and fortitude.	
How do you handle stressful situations?	Show how you stay calm under fire.	
Working with others		
How do you work in teams?	Leader, follower, collaborator -- as appropriate.	

How do you handle conflict?	Show emotional maturity.	
How do you get on with others at work?	Display your teamwork.	

Constraints

Why are you looking for another job?	Tell reasons for leaving.	
What particularly attracted you to this job?	Tell reasons for joining.	
What did you like/dislike about that job?	Show what you learned in both.	
What salary are you seeking?	Understand your value.	

Do you have any questions?

What is a typical day on the job like?	
What do you enjoy about working here the most?	
Why is the position open?	
What skills are you looking for?	
What is the top priority for this position?	
What do you see as challenges for the new employee?	
Can you tell me about the team I would be working with?	
What are the next steps of the hiring process?	

Follow Up

Follow up after an interview

Thank You Notes
- Within 24 hours of the interview
- Be brief and to the point
- Send a note to everyone on the panel
- Restate your interest

Sample Thank You Note

Interviewer (Mr. Smith),

Thank you for the opportunity to interview for (the position), on (date).

I look forward to (an exciting opportunity that we discussed yesterday during the interview) and I am confident that I can exceed your expectations for this position. Meeting your staff and touring your facility reinforced my enthusiasm for the position.

I am very eager to hear back from you with your decision. I can be reached at 123-456-7890.

Sample Email Thank You Note

Good Afternoon Interviewer (Mr. Smith),

Thank you for taking the time to interview me and providing me with a tour this afternoon.

It was great to hear about your (what makes them stand out as an employer). I see this as a great fit for me based on (skills you would like to highlight after completing the interview).

I look forward to discussing this exciting opportunity in more detail. I can be reached at 123-456-7890.

Networking

"It's not what you know, it's who you know." When it comes to finding a job, you've got to network! According to some surveys up to 80% of available jobs are not advertised. These jobs are often referred to as the "hidden job market." This expression is the basis for understanding the importance of networking as a strategy for career development and exploration.
Everyone has a network, even if you don't realize it, and when it comes to job searching, this network may be just as important as your skills and experience.

A personal network is that group of people with whom you interact every day – family, friends, and parents of friends, friends of friends, neighbors, teachers, bosses, and co-workers. With these people, information and experiences are exchanged for both social and potential professional reasons. Networking occurs every time you participate in a school or social event, volunteer in the community, visit with members of your religious group, talk with neighbors, strike up a conversation with someone at the store, or connect with friends online. When networking for the purpose of career development, this means talking with friends, family members, and acquaintances about your goals, your interests, and your dreams. Most people actually learn about job openings through friends, relatives, or others who are part of their personal network, and because each person in your network has a network of his or her own, your potential contacts can grow exponentially. This is important because more often than not, hiring managers would rather talk to a potential candidate who has been recommended by someone they know or already employ. Even if a position is not currently available, networking can lead to informational interviews that can help you not only learn about possible career paths, but can also be great exposure for you to be thought of as a potential candidate when a job opens up.

An informational interview is not the same as a job interview by any means, but it is probably the most effective form of networking there is. In fact, think of it as if, one out of every 20 informational interviews results in a job offer. This is a remarkable number considering the fact that research indicates that only one in every 200 resumes (some studies put the number even higher) results in a job offer.

Use this worksheet as a framework to help develop your story. Remember to cover the 3 Ps – Passion, Previous experience, and Portable/transferable skills.

My career interest/dream is:

_____

I am passionate about this area/industry because:

_____

My related experiences, relevant education or credentials for this field include:

_____

My portable/transferable skills and personal assets (gained through any of your life experiences) related to this field are: _____

_____

End with what you would like to have happen as next steps (although the ideal would be to get the job offer, the goal is to be able to continue the conversation from here):

_____

_____

Communication

Communication skills are important to everyone - they are how we give and receive information and convey our ideas and opinions with those around us.

Communication comes in many forms:
• Verbal (sounds, language, and tone of voice)
• Aural (listening and hearing)
• Non-verbal (facial expressions, body language, and posture)
• Written (journals, emails, blogs, and text messages)
• Visual (signs, symbols, and pictures)

It is important to develop a variety of skills for both communicating *TO* others and learning how to interpret the information received *FROM* others. Knowing our audience and understanding how they need to receive information is equally important as knowing ourselves.

To an employer, good communication skills are essential. In fact, employers consistently rank good communication skills at the top of the list for potential employees.

During an interview, for example, employers are impressed by a job candidate who answers questions with more than one word answers (such as yeah…nah…dunno), demonstrates that he or she is listening, and shares information and ideas (by asking questions for clarification and/or follow up). The interview can be an indication to employers of how the candidate or employee will interact with supervisors, co-workers, and customers or resolve conflicts when they arise. Remember, non-verbal communication is also critical in an interview. Employers expect good eye contact, good posture, and "active" listening.

One of the challenges in the workplace is learning the specific communication styles of others and how and when to share your ideas or concerns. Though some supervisors may specifically ask for your opinion, others may assume if there is something important, they need to know, you will bring it to their attention – or if there is something you are unsure about, you will ask. Knowing how to listen carefully and when to ask for help is important. If an employee and a supervisor learn to communicate well (in whatever method that works), there is a greater likelihood of job retention and promotion.

Now be a star with an example ready to discuss with an employer in an interview. Fill this out to be ready!

Be a STAR

Situation	Task	Action	Result
Describe the background Provide context Where? and When?	Describe the Challenge Problem Expectations	What did you do? How? What tools did you use?	Explain the results Accomplishments Make it measurable

Professionalism

Throughout our working lives, most of us will have many different jobs, each requiring a different level or set of skills. No matter the industry – from customer service to an office job to construction and the trades – all of these jobs have one thing in common: in order to succeed and move ahead, you need to demonstrate *professionalism*. *Professionalism* does not mean wearing a suit or carrying a briefcase; rather, it means conducting oneself with responsibility, integrity, accountability, and excellence. It means communicating effectively and appropriately and always finding a way to be productive.

Employers want new workers to be
- Responsible
- Ethical
- Team oriented
- Possess strong communication, interpersonal and problem-solving skills

Wrap these skills up all together and you've got *professionalism*. As today's labor market becomes more and more competitive, jobseekers will need to continually find ways to stand out from the crowd. There are few things an employer values more than employees who carry out their duties in a professional manner.

Professionalism isn't just one thing: it's a combination of qualities. A professional employee arrives on time for work and manages time effectively. Professional workers take responsibility for their own behavior and work effectively with others. High quality work standards, honesty, and integrity are also part of the package. Professional employees look clean and neat and dress appropriately for the job. Communicating effectively and appropriately for the workplace is also an essential part of professionalism. Regardless of the job or industry, professionalism is easy to spot. On a construction site or in a trade, a professional worker will work hard and manage time effectively, including arriving and returning on time from breaks. A professional worker in a customer service setting will speak clearly and politely to customers and colleagues and have a neat and clean appearance. In an office setting, an employee with professionalism will work productively with others and strive for a high standard and constant improvement. Professionalism may look slightly different in various settings, but the core elements are always the same – and give young employees an edge as they begin their careers.

Be a STAR

Situation	Task	Action	Result
Describe the background Provide context Where? and When?	Describe the Challenge Problem Expectations	What did you do? How? What tools did you use?	Explain the results Accomplishments Make it measurable

Enthusiasm & Attitude

What is the difference between "You're hired!" and "Thank you for your interest, but...?" It can be summed up in one word: *enthusiasm*. *Enthusiasm* can mean the difference between not just getting a job but succeeding in a job and even advancing in your career. A positive and enthusiastic attitude is a critical component of workplace success.

When employers look at prospective candidates, beyond skills, experience, and training, they look for those who demonstrate enthusiasm – those they believe will complete assigned tasks in an upbeat and cooperative manner.

All other things being equal, a candidate who can demonstrate a positive attitude with eagerness to tackle the job will have an advantage over one who displays an attitude viewed by the employer as negative or disinterested.

Managers sometimes worry that this type of person will not get along with supervisors and co-workers, treat customers disrespectfully, and not put much effort into his or her work. On the other hand, employees who are viewed as enthusiastic are known to provide good customer service, resolve interpersonal conflict effectively, and work productively with others.

There are many ways in which an individual might demonstrate enthusiasm in the workplace. For example, in a job interview, he or she might smile, sit up straight, make eye contact, and discuss training and work experiences in an upbeat manner. Once hired into a position, an enthusiastic employee will typically show up on time, show interest in his or her job, and demonstrate a willingness to listen, learn, and try new things. In customer service settings, an enthusiastic employee will approach customers proactively and offer assistance or seek out tasks and projects when there is down time. This positive attitude helps employees go above and beyond to get along with co-workers and managers – even difficult ones – and respond to constructive criticism with maturity and willingness to improve. Overall, an employee with enthusiasm comes across as someone who wants to be at work, and who is willing to do what it takes to get the job done.

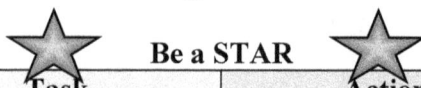

Be a STAR

Situation	Task	Action	Result
Describe the background Provide context Where? and When?	Describe the Challenge Problem Expectations	What did you do? How? What tools did you use?	Explain the results Accomplishments Make it measurable

Teamwork

Teamwork is an essential part of workplace success. Like a basketball team working together to set up the perfect shot, every team member has a specific role to play in accomplishing tasks on the job. Although it may seem as if one player scored the basket, that basket was made possible by many people's planning, coordination, and cooperation to get that player the ball.

Employers look for people who not only know how to work well with others, but who understand that not every player on the team can or will be the one who gets the ball.

When everyone in the workplace works together to accomplish goals, everyone achieves more. The ability to work as part of a team is one of the most important skills in today's job market. Employers are looking for workers who can contribute their own ideas, but also want people who can work with others to create and develop projects and plans.

Teamwork involves building relationships and working with other people using a number of important skills and habits:
• Working cooperatively
• Contributing to groups with ideas, suggestions, and effort
• Communication (both giving and receiving)
• Sense of responsibility
• Healthy respect for different opinions, customs, and individual preferences
• Ability to participate in group decision making

When employees work together to accomplish a goal, everyone benefits. Employers might expect to "see" this in action in different ways. For example, team members in the workplace plan ahead and work cooperatively to assign tasks, assess progress, and deliver on time. They have professional discussions during which, differing approaches and opinions might be shared and assessed in a respectful manner. Even when certain employees end up with tasks that were not their first choices, jobs get done with limited complaints because it is in the spirit of teamwork and with the overall goal in mind.

A leader or manager may often serve as the teamwork facilitator. In this case, team members participate respectfully in discussion, carry out assigned tasks, and defer to the leader in the best interest of the goal. Consensus is wonderful, but not always possible, and an assigned leader will often support and facilitate the decision making necessary for quality teamwork to exist.

Be a STAR

Situation	Task	Action	Result
Describe the background Provide context Where? and When?	Describe the Challenge Problem Expectations	What did you do? How? What tools did you use?	Explain the results Accomplishments Make it measurable

Problem Solving

Everyone experiences problems from time to time. Some of our problems are big and complicated, while others may be more easily solved. There is no shortage of challenges and issues that can arise on the job.

Problem solving and critical thinking refers to the ability to use knowledge, facts, and data to effectively solve problems. This doesn't mean you need to have an immediate answer, it means you have to be able to think on your feet, assess problems and find solutions. The ability to develop a well thought out solution within a reasonable time frame, however, is a skill that employers value greatly.

Employers want employees who can work through problems on their own or as an effective member of a team. Ideal employees can think critically and creatively, share thoughts and opinions, use good judgment, and make decisions. As a new employee, you may question why an organization follows certain steps to complete a task. It may seem to you that one of the steps could be eliminated saving time, effort, and money. However, you may be hesitant to voice your opinion. Don't be. Employers are usually appreciative when new employees are able to offer insight and fresh perspective into better and more efficient ways of doing things. It is important to remember, however, that as someone new to the organization, you may not always have the full picture, and thus there may be factors you are unaware of that dictate things being done in a particular way. Another important thing to remember is that when you are tasked with solving a problem, you don't always need to answer immediately.

⭐ **Be a STAR** ⭐

Situation	Task	Action	Result
Describe the background Provide context Where? and When?	Describe the Challenge Problem Expectations	What did you do? How? What tools did you use?	Explain the results Accomplishments Make it measurable

Do you find yourself overwhelmed by the number and complexity of projects that need to be completed at work each day? As the day flies by, do you often feel as if you haven't paid enough attention to each task because other tasks keep landing on your desk? Do co-workers interrupt you with questions or you can't get it all organized?

You probably know that managing your time effectively will help you get more done each day, but it has important health benefits, too. By managing your time more wisely, you can minimize stress and improve your quality of life. When something comes your way… react with the *5 D's.*

Don't Do It!
There is an option available to us: Not doing the task at all!
The first question one should ask is: What will happen if I don't do this task?
What are the consequences of the task not getting done? Can I live with the consequences? If yes, not doing it is one of the options.

Delay It
Ask the following questions:
Due to time pressure, can the task at hand be delayed?
Can it be done later?
What are consequences of delaying it? Would it be a matter of life and death? Is the task a must do?

Delegate It
One of the ways to get things done is to "*delegate*" it.
This does not mean telling someone to do a task and then forgetting about it. This means taking full responsibility of the work but telling someone else to do it for you. At the same time, you will monitor it and ensure that desired results are achieved.

Dissect It
Instead of doing all at once, dissect the task in smaller steps and get it done in pieces. Just do the tasks you can right now, and you will complete the whole project eventually.
Remember: As the saying goes, "We can eat an elephant one bite at a time or move a mountain one rock at a time." Anthony Robbins has used the word "chunking" for dissection. While learning to drive a car, the "whole" is broken into "parts" and each part is learnt as a separate task. In other words: Divide and rule i.e., divide and get it done.

Do It With Delight
If all the above is not workable, then do the work with enjoyment. Any task which is done with a smile is likely to be executed fast and with passion.

Remember To…
1. Don't waste time.
2. Carry a notebook.
3. Keep a calendar.
4. Work anywhere and everywhere.
5. Break all tasks into small bits.
6. Learn to say no.

Let's Discover a Leader

Now that you are in a position that may point to leadership, let's look at the environment of the workplace. Fellow co-workers searching for the best way to understand others is a difficult process that takes time both as a leader and as an employee, this is time well vested into the relationship that will pay off.

The first step is the ***observation***; ensure that you not only focus on your position, responsibilities and tasks, but also the others around you. If your tasks processed differently, how does that affect the other team members you work with? How can you streamline your responsibilities not only for your benefit, but also to assist the man-hours of project? How you will be rewarded with more individual success? By seeking self and organizational improvement. The payments vary from a higher-level position pay to responsibility upgrades. The question you can ask yourself to start the observation process constructively is not, *"Do you enjoy their company?"* Instead look at this from a professional point of view and ask yourself, *"Does this simplify the process or complex the process?"*

Becoming a leader is the ability to recognize not only a problem area, but also what is causing the problem. Often times the wrong component is replaced, and it is just a matter of time before returning to the problem area and the whole cycle begins again.

Evaluating the staffing is one of the first steps you must conduct in a leadership role to become an effective leader. Observe the staff as a whole. Is it under or overstaffed? What are their qualities, strengths and weaknesses? How is their rapport with each other and with the customers? Is there a balance of the workload? What is the status of the office space? (Is it private enough? Is the information flow as needed? Is it comfortable and ergonomic?) What is the level of knowledge and the experience like? Is there cross training and cross action? Do they have the required tools and resources? How is the mood? You may have to come as a customer or have someone you trust to conduct this survey for you.

> *Leadership is your reaction and action to challenges while professionally providing motivation, direction and purpose to your team*

Another key to success is the ***matter of motivation***; this can be provided in many ways. It may be as simple as time. For example, the single parent working with you has an obligation for their child, but their attendance is not required. However, you have the ability to cover their duties and responsibilities for them and give them that opportunity. They will be motivated to return the favor to you via time, effort or quality. This is just human nature. I was taught young in life that if you simply treat others how you wish to be treated, it will be returned to you without a demand. In other words, find what values you would like. For example, I like to start in the workplace with respect and trust, and by treating others how they would like to be treated. This includes allowing time to pass for the respect to be returned.

The final step is to ***inspire talents***. As a leader, this is something that you have more influence over. This is where you can see the potential in your team members that has never been utilized. This can also be your own talents and how you can bring more to the team. Especially when you see others struggling with a process that is easier for you. Offer your assistance or time in order to complete the project and improve the system.

The only thing left is to move into action. Take any one thing you have discovered and work on a step to find where your passions become your profession. Enjoy all you can in each piece of life to make it whole.

References

Canfield, J., Hansen, M. V., Hewitt, L., & Kasuma, H. (2015). *The power of focus.* Publishing House Sendirian Berhad.

Inc., H. (2021). *Jung Typology Test TM.* Personality test based on C. Jung and I. Briggs Myers type theory. http://www.humanmetrics.com/cgi-win/jtypes2.asp.

O*NET Development, N. C. for. (2021). *O*NET Interest Profiler at My Next Move.* My Next Move. http://www.mynextmove.org/explore/ip.

O*NET Development., N. C. for. (2021). *Build your future with O*NET OnLine.* O*NET OnLine. https://www.onetonline.org/.

O*NET Development., N. C. for. (2021). My Next Move. https://www.mynextmove.org/.

Psychometrics, LLC., T. (2021, February 3). *Myers & Briggs' 16 Personality Types.* Truity. https://www.truity.com/page/16-personality-types-myers-briggs.

Training Administration, U. S. D. of L. E. and. (2019, December 4). *CareerOneStop.* Careers and Career Information. http://www.careeronestop.org/.

University, B. S. (n.d.). *What Careers and Majors Are Right for You?* Myers-Briggs Personality Types. https://www.bsu.edu/about/administrativeoffices/careercenter/tools-resources/personality-types.

www.ingramcontent.com/pod-product-compliance
Lightning Source LLC
Chambersburg PA
CBHW080801300326
41914CB00055B/1017